Hummers,

Knucklers,

and Slow Curves

Contemporary Baseball Poems

◆

Edited by

DON JOHNSON

With a foreword by W. P. Kinsella

University of Illinois Press

◆

Urbana and Chicago

© 1991 by the Board of Trustees of the University of Illinois
Manufactured in the United States of America
1 2 3 4 5 C P 5 4 3 2

This book is printed on acid-free paper.

On the cover: *Minor League* by Clyde Singer, 1964,
Butler Institute of American Art, Youngstown, Ohio.

Library of Congress Cataloging-in-Publication Data

Hummers, knucklers, and slow curves : contemporary baseball poems /
edited by Don Johnson ; with a foreword by W. P. Kinsella.
    p.   cm.
  ISBN 0-252-01810-9 (cl.) — ISBN 0-252-06183-7 (pb.)
  1. Baseball — Poetry.   2. American poetry — 20th century.
I. Johnson, Don, 1942– .
PS595.B33L56   1991
811'.54080355 — dc20   90-48339
                                                           CIP

Hummers,
Knucklers,
and Slow Curves

For my sons,
Matthew and Daniel,
and for my father,
M. R. "Johnny" Johnson.

Contents

◆

Acknowledgments

◆

WILLIAM D. BARNEY. "A Post Card out of Panama" first appeared in *A Literature of Sports*, edited by Tom Dodge. Reprinted by permission of the author.

DAVID BOTTOMS. "Sign for My Father, Who Stressed the Bunt" is reprinted with permission of William Morrow and Co. from *In a U-Haul North of Damascus*. © 1983 by David Bottoms.

NEAL BOWERS. "Late Innings" was first published in *Helicon Nine*, reprinted by author's permission. "World Series Blues" appeared in *Arete* and is reprinted with permission of the author.

RICK CAMPBELL. "Elegy for Richard Hugo from Gainesville" originally appeared in *The Devil's Millhopper* and is reprinted with permission of the author.

DOUGLAS CARLSON. "Russ Joy Little League" first appeared in *The Devil's Millhopper* and is reprinted by permission of the author.

FRED CHAPPELL. "Spitballer," "Junk Ball," and "Strike Zone" are reprinted by permission of Louisiana State University Press from *The World Between the Eyes* by Fred Chappell. © 1963, 1964, 1966, 1969, 1970, and 1971 by Fred Chappell.

TOM CLARK. "Baseball & Classicism," "Baseball," "To Bert Campaneris," and "September in the Bleachers" are reprinted with permission of the author.

GREGORY CORSO. "Dream of a Baseball Star" is reprinted by permission of New Directions Publishing Corp. from *The Happy Birthday of Death*. © 1960 by New Directions Publishing Corp. World rights.

MICHAEL CULROSS. "The Loneliness of the Outfield" and "The Lost Heroes" are reprinted by permission of the University of Pittsburgh Press from *The Lost Heroes*. © 1974 by Michael Culross.

PHILIP DACEY. "Mystery Baseball" is reprinted with permission of The Johns Hopkins University Press from *The Boy under the Bed*. © 1981 by Philip Dacey.

JIM DANIELS. "New Words" and "World Series, 1968" are from *The Long Ball* by Jim Daniels (Pig in a Poke Press, 1988) and are reprinted by permission of the author.

GREGORY DJANIKIAN. "How I Learned English" is reprinted by permission of Carnegie Mellon University Press from *Falling Deeply into America*. © 1989 by Gregory Djanikian. The poem originally appeared in *Poetry*.

RICHARD EBERHART. "Ball Game" is from *Collected Poems 1930–1986*. © 1960, 1976, 1988 by Richard Eberhart. Reprinted by permission of Oxford University Press, Inc.

DAVID ALLEN EVANS. "Will You Sign My Brand-New Baseball, Louie?" is reprinted from *Shenandoah: The Washington and Lee University Review*. © 1974 by Washington and Lee University. It appears here by permission of the editor.

HALVARD JOHNSON. "Americans Playing Slow-Pitch Softball at an Airbase near Kunsan, South Korea" is reprinted by permission of Milkweed Editions from *This Sporting Life: Contemporary Poems About Sports and Games*. © 1987 by Milkweed Editions.

LAURENCE LIEBERMAN. "My Father Dreams of Baseball" is reprinted by permission of Macmillan Publishing Co., Inc., from *The Unbending*. © 1963, 1968 by Laurence Lieberman.

CAROL MASTERS. "Fly Ball" is reprinted by permission of Milkweed Editions from *This Sporting Life: Contemporary Poems About Sports and Games*. © 1987 by Milkweed Editions.

WILLIAM MATTHEWS. "The Hummer" was first published by *The New Republic*. It is reprinted by permission of Little Brown and Co. from *A Happy Childhood*. © 1984 by William Matthews.

GAIL MAZUR. "Baseball" is reprinted by permission of the author from *Nightfire*, David R. Godine Publishers. © 1978 by Gail Mazur. "The Idea of Florida during a Winter Thaw" is printed here by permission of the author.

LINDA MIZEJEWSKI. "Season Wish" is reprinted by permission of the author.

LARRY MOFFI. "Comparative Theology" is reprinted from *A Simple Progression*. © 1981 by Larry Moffi. It appears here through permission of the author.

LILLIAN MORRISON. "When I Was a Kid" first appeared in *Arete* and is reprinted here with permission of the author. "Of Kings and Things" is reprinted from *The Sidewalk Racer and Other Poems of Sports and Motion*. © 1965, 1968, 1977 by Lillian Morrison. All rights reserved. Reprinted by permission of Marian Reiner for the author.

TIM PEELER. "Curt Flood" was published in *The Best of Spitball*, Pocket Books, 1988. It is reprinted by permission of the author.

DONALD PETERSEN. "The Ballad of Dead Yankees" is reprinted by permission of University Press of New England from *The Spectral Boy*. © 1958 by Donald Peterson.

JACK RIDL. "Good Training for Poetry" is reprinted from *Between*, Dawn Valley Press. © 1988 by Jack Ridl. It appears through the author's permission.

MIKE SHANNON. "The Art of Baseball Poetry" originally appeared in *Arete*, and was published in *The Best of Spitball*, Pocket Books, 1988. It is reprinted by permission of the author.

TOM SHEEHAN. "In Cold Fields" was published in *The Best of Spitball*, Pocket Books, 1988. It appears here with permission of the author.

ARTHUR SMITH. "Extra Innings" is reprinted by permission of the University of Pittsburgh Press from *Elegy for Independence Day*. © 1985 by Arthur Smith.

DAVE SMITH. "For Willie Still in Center" and "Mean Rufus Throw Down" are reprinted by permission of the author from *Mean Rufus Throw Down*, Basilisk Press. © 1973 by Dave Smith. "The Roundhouse Voices" originally appeared in *The New Yorker* and is reprinted by permission of the University of Illinois Press from *Goshawk, Antelope*. © 1979 by Dave Smith.

R. T. SMITH. "Softball at Julia Tutwiler Prison" is reprinted by permission of the Water Mark Press from *From the High Dive*. © 1983 by R. T. Smith.

RON SMITH. "Striking Out My Son in the Father-Son Game," from *Running Again in Hollywood Cemetery* (Orlando: University of Central Florida Press), is reprinted by permission of the publisher. © 1988 by Ron Smith.

DABNEY STUART. "Swinging on the First Pitch" is reprinted from *Narcissus Dreaming* with permission of Louisiana State University Press. © 1990 by Dabney Stuart. "Full Count" is reprinted by permission of the author.

Foreword

◆

Poetry has been described as "exact words in perfect order." But to my way of thinking poetry is also about images, about finding ways to present the mundane, the obvious, clothed in words colorful as gift wrapping, offering the reader a vision not seen before, something felt but not quite *known*.

Baseball is poetry. Baseball is ballet. Baseball is chess. Baseball is mystery. Most of all mystery.

In my novel *Shoeless Joe,* Eddie Scissons, an old, dying, fraud of a ballplayer, delivers a sermon from the mound: "The word is baseball," he says. "When you speak the word, something will begin to happen. We underestimate the power of the word . . . I've read the word. I've played it . . . I've digested it . . . when you speak, there is going to be a change in those around you. That is the living word of baseball."

Though I don't write poetry as such, my novels and stories are full of magical happenings, of mystery, of color, of visions built of words. Visions that give the reader a chance to say, "Oh, I've seen that situation a thousand times, but I've never thought of it in quite such a way before. It is as though I've viewed baseball from a new angle, like watching a double play upside down, or looking up at the game from deep in the earth."

As quality poetry should, most of the poems presented here offer their own vision of the world in general and baseball in particular. This volume is filled with imaginative images, with the sight, sound, taste, touch, smell, and mystery of the game. Philip Dacey's poem is worth the price of admission. It is magic realism at its best: invisible players uttering bizarre threats, eerie vendors selling implausible products, players vanishing, others rising in the air as if the Rapture were upon them.

Baseball poetry seems to me a relatively new phenomenon. Did baseball poetry originate with "Casey at the Bat"? I doubt it. But until recently the market for baseball poetry has been virtually nonexistent. Most poetry is published in the literary magazines, which show a bias for esoteric and obscure poetry crammed with large words and classical allusions.

How fortunate we are in recent years to have several quality magazines publishing poetry and prose about baseball. A number of poems in this collection first appeared in *Arete: The Journal of Sport Literature* (recently renamed *Aethlon*). Lyle Olsen and Fred Boe were the driving forces behind *Arete/Aethlon* (now edited by Don Johnson), the first scholarly journal interested in poetry, fiction, and essays on all aspects of sport, not just baseball.

Some of these poems first appeared in *Spitball*, the baseball literary magazine, the brainchild of Mike Shannon of Cincinnati. (No. He never played third base for the Cardinals.) Mike has managed to make *Spitball* survive with little outside financial aid; his dedication to baseball and literature is without parallel in America.

Though not represented in this collection, another fine magazine publishing baseball poetry and fiction is *The Minneapolis Review of Baseball*, founded by Ken La Zebnik.

All three of these magazines have come on the scene within the past ten years, and all have been very supportive of baseball poets and writers.

Baseball, because it is a game of silences, a game of anticipation, is the most literary of sports. True baseball fans have to be thinkers, planners, for the ball is in play for such a short time each game. Baseball fans must use their imaginations to anticipate all the permutations and combinations which might occur the next time the ball is in play.

The open-endedness of baseball makes it a game conducive to poetry and fiction. There is no time limit on a baseball game. Other sports are twice enclosed, first by time, then by rigid playing boundaries. There is no space limit to a baseball game. On a true baseball field the foul lines diverge forever, eventually taking in a good part of the universe. There is theoretically no distance that a great hitter couldn't hit the ball or a great fielder run to retrieve it. In *The Iowa Baseball Confederacy* I have a fielder run from Iowa to New Mexico in pursuit of a fly ball.

Baseball's open-endedness also makes for larger-than-life characters, for the creation of myths and mythology, all of which radiate from these poems with the richness and variety characteristic of contemporary American poetry.

W. P. KINSELLA

Introduction

◆

The poems collected in this volume are as varied, evocative, and mysterious as the game they attempt to describe. Baseball means the American and National leagues, pennant races culminating in contemporary America's version of primitive cultures' autumn harvest festival, the World Series. But baseball is also long bus rides in Class C and D leagues, dusty afternoons in near-empty ballparks in towns such as Elizabethton, Tennessee, or Helena, Montana. Baseball is college ball, high school, American Legion, Babe Ruth and Little League, pickup games in sandlots and pastures, family games of catch in backyards, softball, stickball, tennis-ball-against-the-wall-ball. Surely the game's adaptability accounts to some degree for its enduring popularity. But it doesn't explain our *need* to transform a game meant to be played by eighteen players on a large field into a contest between four kids to a side on a city street, or two imagined teams battling it out in the head of a single youngster throwing a wet tennis ball at a garage door.

These eighty-four poems by fifty-seven American poets go a long way toward providing such an explanation. Individually, they describe baseball's varied forms. In the aggregate, they define its essence.

Although both baseball history and hero worship are revealed here, they occur with less frequency than one might expect, owing in part to my limiting my choices mostly to poems published in the last twenty-five years, after the Dodgers' departure from Brooklyn, after the designated hitter rule, after the breaking of the reserve clause, after baseball's Golden Age. Rhapsodic tributes to the game's giants seem to be the province of prose writers such as Roger Angell, Roger Kahn, and W. P. Kinsella. Our poets tend to take a darker look and to focus on more local conditions. Donald Petersen's "The Ballad of Dead Yankees," written in the fifties, is an exception. Petersen mourns the loss of the great Yankee players of the Babe Ruth era — Lazzeri, Grabowski, Gehrig, and the Babe himself. Yet his lament is itself a tacit admission that the possibilities of heroism were diminishing even in the Eisenhower years.

If our contemporaries are too human, too vulnerable, too much like ourselves, we either look to another era or concentrate on exposing those flaws in our own age which undermine the innocence on which heroism is grounded. Tim Peeler's Curt Flood, for example, is applauded for sacrificing his career for those who came after him, but the poet's assertion that

> you [Flood] are a ghost at barterer's wing,
> your smokey gray eyes
> are two extra zeroes
> on every contract

praises Flood's selflessness while reducing his legacy to purely monetary terms.

In "Mantle," William Heyen records his disappointment at the great Yankee slugger's failure to retire before his diminishing talents tarnished his image. Mantle then sold himself in Brylcreem commercials where "models with open mouths draped around him / as they never were in Commerce, Oklahoma," where he grew up. Heyen takes the reader back to Mantle's boyhood, back to the workouts with his father who trained the young prospect to switch hit:

> his father winged them in,
> and the future blew toward him
>
> now a fastball, now a slow
> curve hanging
> like a model's smile,

suggesting that the seeds for Mantle's corruption were planted early on in the fertile soil of that Oklahoma barnyard.

Other major league stars make appearances of varying length and importance in these poems, from "cup of coffee" stints by Babe Ruth, Ted Williams, and Carl Yastrzemski in Gail Mazur's "The Idea of Florida during a Winter Thaw," to "pinch hitting" by Bobby Murcer, Louie Aparicio, Lou Brock, Bob Gibson, Don Wert, and Willie Mays in poems by Rodney Torreson, David Allen Evans, Jim Daniels, and Dave Smith. There are also "complete games" by Whitey Ford and Bert Campaneris in poems named for them by Jonathan Holden and Tom Clark, respectively. But the poem that most powerfully chronicles the disappearance of heroism and poignantly epitomizes our almost desperate need for baseball heroes, despite our recognition of their vulnerability, is Gregory Corso's "Dream of a Baseball Star." Corso features Ted Williams in a cosmic baseball confrontation

> flinging his schoolboy wrath
> toward some invisible pitcher's mound
> —waiting the pitch all the way from heaven.

The pitches come by the hundreds, "all afire," but Williams goes down swinging and Corso's speaker cries out in his dream:

> God! throw thy merciful pitch!
> Herald the crack of bats!
> Hooray the sharp liner to left!
> Yea the double, the triple!
> Hosannah the home run!

Obviously, more is going on here than just a mythical face-off between batter and pitcher. When Williams, the perennial bad boy (Corso, following the lead of Randall Jarrell, also calls him a poet), openly flaunts the Ultimate Fireballer but fails to connect, the dreamer asks for mercy, not merely for Williams, but for the rest of us as well.

Surprisingly, it is not the game's heroes, but the game itself which preoccupies most of the poets represented here. Many of them write in first person from personal experience, but almost as many offer more objective analyses of the game as a whole or of specific plays or positions. Rolfe Humphries is a spectator to a well-played "Night Game" which restores his sense of belonging in the world. Leaving the ballpark, he exclaims, "*Oh this is good,* to be part of this movement, / This mood, this music, part of the human race." Jonathan Holden describes the bucolic essence of the game in "How to Play Night Baseball," and in both "World Series Blues" and "Baseball: Divine Comedy," Neal Bowers and Robert A. Fink, respectively, record the way in which our seasonal expectations and disappointments are bound up within the game.

In a consistently ironic denial of the popular cliché, Gail Mazur in "Baseball" declares that "The game of baseball is not a metaphor / and I know it's not really life." But despite her recurrent assertions that the game is not a microcosm, she provides enough examples of parallels between game and life to undercut her premise with evidence. The ballpark

> is an artifact,
> manicured, safe, "scene in an Easter egg,"
> and the order of the ball game,
> the firm structure with the mystery
> of accidents always contained,

and it is "not the wild field we wander in" in life. But the players' striving for excellence, their inexplicable slumps, the lack of involvement of some of the spectators, the violent tendencies of others, the ultimate mystery that informs the game make it, if not a metaphor, at least a synecdoche for life.

The enigmatic quality of baseball, the mystery alluded to above, is the subject of several of these poets. Perhaps the game's association with seasonal change (spring training means the real end of winter and the World Series marks the beginning of autumn), its reliance on ritual, and the role fate and chance seem to play in particular games, seasons, or decades account for this emphasis. Whatever the reason, both John Updike and James Tate suggest parallels between baseball and Asian religions or philosophies, and Susan Firer, in the middle of the Saint Mary of Czestochowa's annual kielbasa festival, remembers the women she has played with and the plays they have made or not made, and becomes "homesick for Oshkosh women's softball" and is mysteriously drawn back to "A Night Game in Menomonie Park." Larry Moffi characterizes his poem about a long-suffering Cubs fan as "a lesson in theology," and in "A Personal History of the Curveball" Jonathan Holden repeats the word "magic" four times within seven lines to describe the movement of a particular roundhouse curve that fooled him.

The underlying mystery in baseball is most fully articulated, however, in William Heyen's "The Stadium" and Philip Dacey's "Mystery Baseball." In the former, Heyen creates an apocalyptic situation in which the moon fails to appear for three nights in a row. Sensing their impending doom, crowds gather in the stadium and integrate ceremonies of innocence and religious ritual into a baseball setting. "Children run the bases" while those in the stands sing hymns, then file down to the infield grass where "makeshift communion rails" have been erected. What clinches the connection between religion and baseball is Heyen's assertion that

> We've known all our lives
> that we would gather here in the stadium
> on just such a night.

Unconsciously, we have known that our association with baseball would bring us to the stadium for reasons that lie beyond its mere capacity to accommodate the supplicants gathered in search of revelation and deliverance.

Focusing on the mysteries inherent *in* the game, rather than its religious overtones, Philip Dacey creates a series of myths that accumulate to establish baseball's preternatural essence. The man who throws out the first ball of the season is a mysterious stranger. Each team fields an invisible tenth player so that

> Runners edging off base feel a tap on their shoulders,
>   turn, see no one.
> Or a batter, the count against him, will hear whispered
>   in his ear vague, dark
> rumors of his wife, and go down.

Pitchers look everywhere for signs; a runner disappears after rounding third, and, in a scene reminiscent of a Gabriel García Márquez novel, an outfielder leaps for a fly ball and simply keeps ascending, only to come to earth days later, to wander dazed in the outfield. Dacey's final image suggests both knowledge and complicity on the part of the players of the game. He describes an old man who lives "deep under second base," whose presence the players acknowledge throughout the game by pulling at their caps. Dacey suggests that baseball is fundamentally mysterious, that what goes on in the game spectators applaud is tied to roots the layman can only guess at.

Other poets concentrate on specific aspects of the game or the play at a particular position. Fred Chappell's "Spitballer," "Junk Ball," and "Strike Zone" all display specific knowledge of the game; and "Spitballer," with its concluding observation that the thrower of wet ones draws a second salary as a groundskeeper "since while he pitches he waters the lawn," reveals Chappell's rich comic sensibility and awareness of baseball humor. Dabney Stuart's "Full Count" is similar to "Junk Ball," and also displays the humorous side of the game with the hitter fouling everything off, the catcher curling up at the umpire's feet to nap, and the "blind" umpire mistaking the catcher for his dog and assuming that "the game's over and he's back / on his porch in his rocking chair." When the umpire begins to tell a story, the stands and benches empty. The players mill around, talking and chewing together, and they remain there, the count three-and-two, waiting.

Robert Francis's poems are also somewhat similar to Chappell's, focusing as they do on the play of one player as in "Pitcher" and "The Base Stealer." "Pitcher" shares one other trait with Chappell's "Spitballer" and illustrates one of the anthology's most significant leitmotifs — the relationship between baseball and poetry. Through his close description of the pitcher's actions Francis strongly suggests a parallel between the pitcher and the poet. The pitcher's "art is eccentricity," as is the poet's. They work through indirection, seeking "to avoid the obvious." "Every seeming aberration" of both is "willed," and while the poet hopes to slip into the reader's mind almost without that reader's awareness, the pitcher strives to make "the batter understand too late."

The link between baseball and writing was first articulated by Marianne Moore in "Baseball and Writing," and in addition to Chappell's and Francis's poems is picked up in this collection by Jack Ridl in "Good Training for Poetry," by Mike Shannon in "The Art of Baseball Poetry," by Richard Jackson in "Center Field," by Arthur Smith in "Extra Innings," and by Dave Smith in "The Roundhouse Voices." By extension it is also a factor in sevral poems that emphasize the language associated with baseball, as in Jim Daniels's "New Words," and in Gregory Djanikian's "How I Learned English," in which the immigrant boy's assimilation into this culture is recorded in his ability to pick up the language of baseball. After struggling with the game and its language Djanikian's speaker recalls how he settled into his position

> Tugging at my cap in just the right way,
> Crouching low, my feet set,
> "Hum baby" sweetly on my lips.

Although Djanikian's use of baseball as a means of the young boy's integration into American culture is unique among these poems because the boy is a newly arrived immigrant, the idea of baseball as a vehicle for the formation of a child's identity is one of the most common threads connecting the poems of this collection. These poems tend to be the most personal: reminiscences of particular games or moments, memories of lessons taught by fathers or father surrogates, images of friends and teammates. Since baseball, more than any other of our games, is dependent on memory, and the poet's "assignment is to remember," as Halvard Johnson reminds us, it is in these poems that baseball and poetry achieve their most perfect union.

Many of these pieces involve children or revolve around memories of childhood. "In Cold Fields" is Tom Sheehan's recollection of being left behind "in our sneakers / and innocence" by the big brothers, "all the long-ball hitters," who went off to fight in World War II, the younger brothers evolving and maturing so that when the Korean War occurred they, by now the heavy hitters, went off and "left our brothers / on corners, in cold fields." Lillian Morrison recalls playing stickball in Jersey City, New Jersey, in a poem that gives the lie to the axiom that it is "always fathers and sons." Along with Morrison, Conrad Hilberry, Jack Ridl, and Linda Mizejewski explore the possibilities for fathers and daughters as well.

All three of Richard Hugo's poems are memory pieces. Even though "Missoula Softball Tournament" is written in present tense, it unfolds against the speaker's admission that in coming to the tournament he has "gone back to the old ways of defeat, / the softball field, familiar dust and thud." But it is in "Letter to Mantsch from Havre" and "From Altitude, the Diamonds" that the past most fully impinges on the present in Hugo's baseball poems. In the former the poet returns to Havre where the team he had played on had been beaten by a local pitcher who was the town barber. What stuck in the poet's mind, however, was not the defeat, but the four home runs, the triple and the single that his teammate Mike Mantsch had hit in the three-game series. In a world that rarely allows unabashed praise, Mantsch's performance stands out because "it is our pleasure / to care about something well done."

In "From Altitude . . . " memories of a whole life in baseball are triggered by the ubiquitous baseball diamonds one sees from airplanes flying over this country. In this case, though, the "memories" are the product of wish fulfillment on the part of the speaker. He is creating a past in which his baseball triumphs and failures represent the victories and defeats of his life as a whole. Adopting the second-person point of view, Hugo says, "You've played on every one," blending observations about his own present state (fat, bald, anxious about flying) with what might be called nostalgic fantasies which, the reader understands, cannot be historically true: You "tripled home / the run" to beat the Sox in Chicago; you pitched a great game in the Bronx, ultimately losing to "that left-hander, / Ford, who made it big. . . . "

Hugo's second-person narrator coupled with the diverse and varied nature of the experiences he describes while flying across the United States creates an American Everyman who, as his plane descends toward a landing, focuses in upon another ballpark, with runners rounding third, driven home by a triple, the hitter,

> his lungs filled with the cheers of those
> he has loved forever, on his magnificent tiny way
> to an easy stand-up three.

Life goes on. Vitality is renewed in each game on all those highly recognizable diamonds that decorate the landscape.

Memory is the central issue in Arthur Smith's "Extra Innings," in which the speaker recalls that the ballpark grass of his youth was so

> sweet-smelling, I think
> I could have bellied down near the dugout
> And drowsed away the afternoon.

Against this background of pastoral innocence, he recalls breaking up the no-hitter of a young man who turns out to have been Tom Seaver. But then the speaker questions the validity of his reminiscence, thinking that Seaver, looking back, would remember a no-hitter accomplished, the last out being a strikeout, and that the left fielder might recall saving the game with a shoestring catch for the last out. Smith, like Hugo, asserts that the facts are not as important as our memories, which create our own reality. We try to

> accommodate
> what happened with what
> Might have happened. And it never turns out true,
>
> The possibilities not to be trusted but, rather,
> Believed in against the facts — whatever they are.

We are the sum total of the memories of what we were, but we create those memories, our myths of ourselves.

Sometimes the juxtaposition of what we thought we were becoming with what we actually are generates a bitter reaction, as is the case with Dave Smith's speaker in "The Roundhouse Voices." Coming home for the funeral of an uncle who had coached him in childhood baseball games, he visits the railroad roundhouse where those games took place. As a youngster he would sneak into the railyard to meet his uncle, much to the chagrin of the company guard who strove to keep the young boy out. The uncle inspired the boy, encouraged him to aspire to perfection, and urged him to taunt the guard, who plays an increasingly sinister role as the poem develops, coming ultimately to represent death. Charged with hope and innocence, the boy sets out to conquer the world only to be betrayed by the uncle who himself succumbs to death, thus undermining all the lessons the young man learned as a boy in the roundhouse.

Death lurks at the edges of many of these poems, probably because most sports poems are ultimately about loss: loss of face, loss of games, loss of youth and vitality, and death is the ultimate loss. But loss is what makes love meaningful, because it deprives us of those things that we most cherish, most want to retain. Love, on the other hand, is what makes death so difficult. If we did not love we would not be as reluctant to leave those we know or have them leave us. Richard Jackson explores the relationship between love and death in a baseball setting in "Center Field." As he waits for a long fly ball to drop out of the darkness into his glove, he thinks of all his close friends and former teammates who have died. He writes:

> I am trying to remember anyone I have loved,
> and it turns out it was usually too late, that we stood
> like embarrassed batters caught looking at a third strike.

After recording all those who have gone down, Jackson declares that

> this is a poem
> that could go on being about either death or love,
> and we have only the uncertain hang time
> of a fly ball to decide how to position ourselves,
> to find the right words for our love,
> to turn towards home as the night falls, as the ball,
> as the loves, the deaths we grab for our own.

Ultimately, all these poems are attempts "to find the right words for our love," for our love of those first green fields we played in, the fathers and mothers and uncles who coached us, and the heroes who inspired us even while betraying us by growing old. Although the poems record more losses than victories, more disappointments than celebrations, they testify to the power of our expectations, the strength of our dreams. If we did not invest so much in our games, the chronicles of our losses could not be infused with enough vigor and poignancy to inspire the next generation of players.

Hummers,
Knucklers,
and Slow Curves

William D. Barney
A Post Card out of Panama

◆

The young man at the plate, bat bristling,
studies us in a hazel calm.
Whatever world and wind serve up,
he'll meet it. Just the right aplomb,
none of that sneering, Casey-like,
how he'll unseam the white horse-hide.
He knows his muscle and his eye
feed on a fast one, high, inside.

It turns out he's not up to hit;
the thing is history: on the back
in a bold script tough as his swing
he writes, and you can hear it crack:
"After I'd hit the longest drive
ever seen on the Isthmus." He is proud.
I hear that jungle-bordered park,
the roar going up from a wild crowd.

He had a thin time growing up,
but once filled out, he made a man;
tasted some triumphs, and more losses,
he lived clean as the strongest can.
Look at him, come to his high hour,
leaning his body toward the pitch
with every sinew, bone and cell alive —
my father was exceedingly rich.

David Bottoms

Sign for My Father,
Who Stressed the Bunt

◆

On the rough diamond,
the hand-cut field below the dog lot and barn,
we rehearsed the strict technique
of bunting. I watched from the infield,
the mound, the backstop
as your left hand climbed the bat, your legs
and shoulders squared toward the pitcher.
You could drop it like a seed
down either base line. I admired your style,
but not enough to take my eyes off the bank
that served as our center-field fence.

Years passed, three leagues of organized ball,
no few lives. I could homer
into the garden beyond the bank,
into the left-field lot of Carmichael Motors,
and still you stressed the same technique,
the crouch and spring, the lead arm absorbing
just enough impact. That whole tiresome pitch
about basics never changing,
and I never learned what you were laying down.

Like a hand brushed across the bill of a cap,
let this be the sign
I'm getting a grip on the sacrifice.

Neal Bowers

Late Innings

◆

for Marianne Moore

Bucking and bolting before the hurrying dark,
the boys in the field across the road could be ponies,
they are so lost in the thoughtless art of being themselves.

Playing in the drained light of a sun already set,
they chase something so hard to see
it might be imaginary but for the snap
against wood, the smack on leather.

Their makeshift bases of tin scraps and cardboard
are the fading points of a dying star,
but still they cry for one more turn at bat,
crouching for the pitch coming out of nowhere.

In the west, the sky flares its dull embers,
grows luminous beyond the horizon as if the lights
in a distant stadium had been switched on,
and the last boy digs in at home with the crickets,
the gathering dew, waiting for the long, dark curve.

World Series Blues

◆

Summer always looks good in spring training,
sometimes showing up early
to get into shape for the long season,
playing the exhibition schedule so well
you can't help thinking this is the year
to go all the way.

Even in the city, where cold
hangs on through April in gray block and cement,
you have to feel hopeful, seeing the sun hit
farther into the outfield bleachers,
higher and higher every day, with power.

But then comes the solstice,
the inevitable slump and scramble to hold on
to what seemed to be a perfect season,
with fatigue setting in, the lights coming on
a little earlier each evening,
and a definite chill in the air.

Anyone could guess this series won't go seven games,
the way the opposing team sprints out
in crisp, white uniforms to take the field,
ready to play hardball.

Rick Campbell

Elegy for Richard Hugo
from Gainesville

◆

I want to say to a world that feels
with reason it has little chance, well done.

— Richard Hugo
"Letter to Mantsch from Havre"

I will not say there is anything good in this,
will not talk of metaphysics
or heaven. I want to live in this world
like it's the only one. Live
where the morning moon glides
like a hawk. Walk along the coast
below Big Sur and watch
breakers swell like blue whales.
Look down over brown cliffs
at the white, twisting strip of sand.
Stand on the Bridge of the Americas
and watch tankers steam into the Pacific.
Or just stay home,
knowing that the dogwoods will break out singing,
that the sky here couldn't be bluer
for blood or money. Stand in early February
without my shirt, in the good green of centerfield,
hear the crack and break for the fence,
leap high and backhand one going over.
For you friend, for you.

Douglas Carlson
Russ Joy Little League

◆

God help me, liberal mothers,
I'm trying not to be competitive:

standing apart from the screaming others,
a quiet smile on my lips, bemused,
watching children play, striking
the pose of former athlete
reduced to jogging and tennis,
thickening around the middle.

But there we are, Kevin, you
are two-for-two; I am oh-for-thirty-seven,
last inning, runner on second.

You take the first pitch for a strike;
the banshees howl from the bleachers
and a small word passes through your
half smile. But you are angry with
yourself, not the umpire. I'm just proud.

The second pitch is high;
you swing in anger as I
would have done. Now we have
two strikes on us.
I'm trying not to be competitive,
but we must protect the plate:
two strikes, two outs,
last inning, the sun is in our eyes.
There will be better times than these.

Now I want to be with you
in our fantasies: a compact, level

swing, the ball sailing like a gull
out and over the falling sun
to a jetty where we sit growing older,
not competing with fish we never catch.

Fred Chappell

Spitballer

◆

A poet because his hand goes first
to his head & then to his heart.

The catcher accepts the pitch
as a pool receives a dripping diver;
soaks up the curve like
cornflakes in milk.

The hitter makes great
show of wringing out his bat.

On the mound he grins, tiger
in a tree, when the umpire
turns round & round the ball
magically dry as alum.

He draws a second salary as maintenance man.
Since while he pitches he waters the lawn.

Junk Ball

◆

By the time it gets to the plate
it's got weevils and termites.

Trying to hit Wednesday with a bb gun.

Sunday.

Or curves like a Chippendale leg or
flutters like a film unsprocketed or
plunges like Zsa Zsa's neckline or
sails away as coy as Shirley Temple

(or)

Not even Mussolini could make
the sonofabitch arrive on time.

Strike Zone

◆

for Joe Nicholls

Like the Presidency its size
depends upon the man.

Paneless window he doesn't want to smash,
the pitcher whittles at the casement.

The batter peers
into it like a peeping tom.
Does he like what he sees?

The limits get stricter
as they get less visible:

throwing at yards & yards of McCovey,
an inch or so
of Aparicio,
the pitcher tries not to go
bats.

The umpire knows a secret.
But he gives no sign.

Ball 2.

Tom Clark

Baseball & Classicism

◆

Every day I peruse the box scores for hours
Sometimes I wonder why I do it
Since I am not going to take a test on it
And no one is going to give me money

The pleasure's something like that of codes
Of deciphering an ancient alphabet say
So as brightly to picturize Eurydice
In the Elysian Fields on her perfect day

The day she went 5 for 5 against Vic Raschi

Baseball

◆

One day when I was studying with Stan Musial, he pointed out
that one end of the bat was fatter than the other. "This end is
more important than the other," he said. After twenty years I
learned to hold the bat by the handle. Recently, when Willie
Mays returned from Europe, he brought me a German bat of
modern make. It can hit any kind of ball. Pressure on the shaft
at the end near the handle frees the weight so that it can be
retracted or extended in any direction. A pitcher came with
the bat. The pitcher offers not one but several possibilities.
That is, one may choose the kind of pitch one wants. There
is no ball.

To Bert Campaneris

◆

You've had your problems
over the years but when
the money's on the table
you come out smokin', Campy
You didn't have to go through all this atavism, you know

You could have stayed home and made lariats in the rope
    factory like your father
but you went away to the big leagues
for $500
and on your first time up even though your English was bad
you hit a home run
and that made Charley Finley happy
and after he made you play all nine positions in one game for a joke
he made you his shortstop for life
meaning until your legs start to go
which I hope isn't soon
since I love the way you play the field
with a cool mechanical glide
and intensely run the bases
so diminutive and severe

We're both 35
and you're earning 100 grand now
and looking for a five year contract
and I'm getting a hundred bucks
for doing this poetry reading

Which I guess just goes to show
how good you know English
don't count for everything

September in the Bleachers

♦

In the bathroom the bad dudes
are putting money on Ali & Kenny Norton
up & down the row of stalls
little coveys of guys with tiny radios
callin out the blow by blow:
Round two to Muhammad! Whoo!

I listen to all this while I'm pissing
& the national anthem's playing outside
then make it back up thru the hot dog line
to catch the first inning, grinning,
my heart tells me Vida will shut out Kansas City tonight.

He goes right ahead & does it before my eyes.

Gregory Corso

Dream of a Baseball Star

◆

I dreamed Ted Williams
leaning at night
against the Eiffel Tower, weeping.

He was in uniform
and his bat lay at his feet
— knotted and twiggy.

"Randall Jarrell says you're a poet!" I cried.
"So do I! I say you're a poet!"

He picked up his bat with blown hands;
stood there astraddle as he would in the batter's box,
and laughed! flinging his schoolboy wrath
toward some invisible pitcher's mound
— waiting the pitch all the way from heaven.

It came; hundreds came! all afire!
He swung and swung and swung and connected not one
sinker curve hook or right-down-the-middle.
A hundred strikes!

The umpire dressed in strange attire
thundered his judgment: YOU'RE OUT!
And the phantom crowd's horrific boo
dispersed the gargoyles from Notre Dame.

And I screamed in my dream:
God! throw thy merciful pitch!
Herald the crack of bats!
Hooray the sharp liner to left!
Yea the double, the triple!
Hosannah the home run!

Michael Culross

4. The Loneliness of the Outfield

From
"The Bushleaguers"

◆

19 innings, no chances accepted — August 12, 1947

They never liked me
at the Milwaukee
park — that day the left
field stands were filled with
hecklers who pelted

me with catcalls and
empty beer cans; but
they tired in the
extra innings, and
most of them left. I

began to daydream
routine fly balls, line
drive doubles, a game-
losing error. But
I disappointed

the few who stayed to
the finish: their team
somehow managed to
lose it without me.

The Lost Heroes

♦

*Not many major leaguers came
out of the Rocky Mountains.*
— Curt Gowdy

The exhibition at Pocatello
Had gone smoothly enough: three quick runs
In the second were all they needed;
After that, most of the regulars

Watched from the dugout. Another easy
Win, but their bus from Boise was late.
When it finally arrived, only
The trainer and Kurtz, the first baseman

Showed up at the station to take it.
The others, whether victims of foul
Play, or lured off by some fabled
Trout stream, were never seen again, although

The front office continues to hope
Signed contracts for next year will turn up.

1965

Philip Dacey
Mystery Baseball

◆

No one knows the man who throws out the season's first ball.
   His face has never appeared in the newspapers,
      except in crowd scenes, blurred.
   Asked his name, he mumbles something
      about loneliness,
      about the beginnings of hard times.

Each team fields an extra, tenth man.
   This is the invisible player,
      assigned to no particular position.
   Runners edging off base feel a tap on their shoulders,
      turn, see no one.
   Or a batter, the count against him, will hear whispered
      in his ear vague, dark
      rumors of his wife, and go down.

Vendors move through the stands
   selling unmarked sacks,
   never disclosing their contents,
   never having been told.
   People buy, hoping.

Pitchers stay busy
   getting signs.
   They are everywhere.

One man rounds third base, pumping hard,
   and is never seen again.
   Teammates and relatives wait years at the plate,
      uneasy, fearful.

An outfielder goes for a ball on the warning track.
   He leaps into the air and keeps rising,

[18]

beyond himself, past
the limp flag.
Days later he is discovered,
   descended, wandering dazed
   in centerfield.

Deep under second base lives an old man,
   bearded, said to be
a hundred. All through the game,
players pull at the bills of their caps,
acknowledging him.

Jim Daniels
New Words

◆

Saturday afternoon, alone in the living room
I crouched on the floor to watch
the Tigers lose another game.

Don Wert let a ball roll through
his legs and down the line in left.
You pimp, I cried
as the winning run scored.

My mother dropped laundry, grabbed my arm:
what'd you call him?
Pimp, I mumbled. I was nine
and about to learn a new word.

My mother turned off the tv.
A man sells a woman's body.
I thought about that for a long time:

Don Wert missed a ground ball.
Don Wert did not sell women's bodies.
Don Wert was not a good third baseman.
Don Wert was not a pimp.

It would be a couple more years
before I thought much about women's bodies
before I etched a g for girls
into my dresser drawer knob I used
to dial in my dreams.

That night I pinned Don Wert's baseball card
to my dartboard and took my pleasure.
Pimp, I whispered, *pimp*.

World Series, 1968

◆

My mother's friend Angie from work
knew how much I liked baseball
and gave me the ticket she got
from Vic Wertz, the beer distributor
for the wedding hall her mother ran.
Angie gave me allergy shots every week —
she was beautiful in her white uniform.

I went with her fiance, who didn't know much
about baseball. I was twelve, caught
between sports and the sexual wake-up call.
Art was his name, and as we sat
in left field box seats, upper deck,
I wished Angie were with me instead.
I bought ginger ale and shivered.
He drank beer and shivered.
The Tigers lost 10–1. Lou Brock's stolen bases.
Bob Gibson's strikeouts. The wind blasted
our faces. He wanted to leave early
but I wouldn't budge. I kept whispering
The World Series, The World Series . . .
but I was still cold.

Gregory Djanikian
How I Learned English

◆

It was in an empty lot
Ringed by elms and fir and honeysuckle.
Bill Corson was pitching in his buckskin jacket,
Chuck Keller, fat even as a boy, was on first,
His T-shirt riding up over his gut,
Ron O'Neill, Jim, Dennis, were talking it up
In the field, a blue sky above them
Tipped with cirrus.
                    And there I was,
Just off the plane and plopped in the middle
Of Williamsport, Pa. and a neighborhood game,
Unnatural and without any moves,
My notions of baseball and America
Growing fuzzier each time I whiffed.

So it was not impossible that I,
Banished to the outfield and daydreaming
Of water, or a hotel in the mountains,
Would suddenly find myself in the path
Of a ball stung by Joe Barone.
I watched it closing in
Clean and untouched, transfixed
By its easy arc before it hit
My forehead with a thud.
                          I fell back,
Dazed, clutching my brow,
Groaning, "Oh my shin, oh my shin,"
And everybody peeled away from me
And dropped from laughter, and there we were
All of us writhing on the ground for one reason
Or another.
              Someone said "shin" again,
There was a wild stamping of hands on the ground,
A kicking of feet, and the fit

Of laughter overtook me too,
And that was important, as important
As Joe Barone asking me how I was
Through his tears, picking me up
And dusting me off with hands like swatters,
And though my head felt heavy,
I played on till dusk
Missing flies and pop-ups and grounders
And calling out in desperation things like
"Yours" and "take it," but doing all right,
Tugging at my cap in just the right way,
Crouching low, my feet set,
"Hum baby" sweetly on my lips.

Richard Eberhart

Ball Game

◆

Caught off first, he leaped to run to second, but
Then struggled back to first.
He left first because of a natural desire
To leap, to get on with the game.
When you jerk to run to second
You do not necessarily think of a home run.
You want to go on. You want to get to the next stage,
The entire soul is bent on second base.
The fact is that the mind flashes
Faster in action than the muscles can move.
Dramatic! Off first, taut, heading for second,
In a split second, total realization,
Heading for first. Head first! Legs follow fast.
You struggle back to first with victor effort
As, even, after a life of effort and chill,
One flashes back to the safety of childhood,
To that strange place where one had first begun.

David Allen Evans

"Will You Sign My Brand-New Baseball, Louie?"

◆

the best thing in my head
of baseball and Kansas City
is the Royals playing the
Red Sox and the drunk trying
to get Louie Aparicio
to sign his brand-new baseball:
every time Louie comes loping in
from shortstop at the end
of the half inning there he is
the drunk elbowing his way
from high up in the grandstand
down into the box seats and all
those turned-around wrinkled
foreheads and goddammits and
uplifted cups of Hamms and
Dr. Pepper with amazing
timing to catch his man
exactly at the screen except
that Louie every time
fields with his eyes that
white routine ball coming
out of the crowd and drops
his look and speeds up just
a little then disappears
into the dugout safe as the
fans cheer and cheer and
cheer for both of their heroes

Charles Fanning

Stickball at Charlestown High

◆

September 1975

The scoring is easy.
The eye-level ledge
and above is a single.
The second and third floors
are doubles and triples.
A homerun is hitting
the name of the school.
That is, if the ball isn't caught.
The street is an out.

The ball is a half-ball,
cut from cheap rubber
and hollow.
The wind in its core
makes it whistle
and gives it a natural curve.
The bat is a broomstick
or thinner.
On both sides the game
is all in the wrists.

Everyone over thirty here
is overweight on beer.
The night streets run with piss
on Bunker Hill,
from the misplaced monument on top
to the project at the bottom.
On weekends men fold rage
in liquid cotton,
then beat each other's heads in
with the bottles,
while women pray in parlours
strewn with last year's palms

to pictures
of the Sacred Heart of Jesus.

This fine soft day
the smack and swish of sticks
breaks tensions
like a fart takes belly cramps.
Watching the cut ball
skid across the darkening face
of their high school
are families in lawn chairs
in the street.
There is no traffic
and the kids are safe.
Today is Sunday.

Robert A. Fink

In Case You Thought
They Played for Money

◆

Next Saturday catch Baseball's Game of the Week.
Study the man in right,
the forgotten one who dreams
of left-handed teams, all
pull hitters who send him deep
to make the leaping snag,
glove always just above the wall.
Young women smile behind their hands.
The Commissioner's mother phones to say
an apple pie is cooling on the sill,
she's set an extra place for dinner.

Baseball: Divine Comedy

◆

"You count on it [baseball],
   rely on it to buffer the passage of time,
   to keep the memory of sunshine and high skies
   alive, and then just when the days
   are twilight, when you need it most,
   it stops."
          Angelo Bartlett Giamatti 1938–1989

1.

It breaks your heart,
this game you call your life,
no less than the first girl
you lay back with in a green field
and named the high, white shapes
you knew were only clouds
and how they turn
when the wind shifts north,
the chill rains come.

      "I can still run and catch
      the fly in center field."
          A. Bartlett Giamatti

2.

Dante would have chosen center —
a man cast farthest out, poised
on the invisible seam
that splits the diamond into wings
he springs to lift
each time a line drive starts to climb.

[29]

"Southward goes the wind,
then turns to the north; it turns
and turns again; then back
to its circling goes the wind."
Ecclesiastes 1 : 6

3.

Only a man of vision
dare play this far from home,
a man of grace, of noble mien,
whose faith is in the solid
crack of ash, the high fly's course
against the azure dome.
He charts, with glee,
the multifoliate levels of the wind.

Susan Firer

A Night Game in Menomonie Park

◆

A night game in Menomonie Park,
Where the ladies hit the large white balls
like stars through the night they roll
like angelfood cake batter folded through devilsfood.
Again, I want to hear the fans' empty beer cans
being crushed — new ones hissing open.
"You're a gun, Anna"
"She can't hit"
"Lay it on."
Oh, run, swift softball women
under the lights the Kiwanis put in.
Be the wonderful sliding night
animals I remember. Remind me constantly
of human error and redemption.
Hit
ball after ball to the lip of the field
while the lake flies fall like confetti
under the park's night lights.
Sunlight Dairy Team, remember me
as you lift your bats,
pump energy into
them bats, whirling circular as helicopter
blades above your heads.
Was it the ball Julie on the Honey "B" Tavern Team
hit toward my head that made me so soft-
ball crazy that right in the middle of a tune
by Gentleman Jim's Orchestra, here in Bingo/Polka
Heaven at Saint Mary of Czestochowa's annual Kielbasa
Festival, I go homesick for Oshkosh women's softball?
I order another Kielbasa and wonder
if Donna will stay on third next game or
again run head down wild into Menomonie homeplate.
Play louder, Gentleman Jim.
Saint Mary of Czestochowa throws a small festival, but
Oshkosh women's softball — that's a whole other ballgame.

Robert Francis

Pitcher

◆

His art is eccentricity, his aim
How not to hit the mark he seems to aim at,

His passion how to avoid the obvious,
His techique how to vary the avoidance.

The others throw to be comprehended. He
Throws to be a moment misunderstood.

Yet not too much. Not errant, arrant, wild,
But every seeming aberration willed.

Not to, yet still, still to communicate
Making the batter understand too late.

The Base Stealer

◆

Poised between going on and back, pulled
Both ways taut like a tightrope-walker,
Fingertips pointing the opposites,
Now bouncing tiptoe like a dropped ball
Or a kid skipping rope, come on, come on,
Running a scattering of steps sidewise,
How he teeters, skitters, tingles, teases,
Taunts them, hovers like an ecstatic bird,
He's only flirting, crowd him, crowd him,
Delicate, delicate, delicate, delicate — now!

Robert Gibb

Baseball

♦

for Richard Gaughran

Vivaldi would have loved it,
The way every movement conduces to
The season's general fugue.

He had the mind for such things
As happen together
                              and are resolved
Through patterns of play.

Multiplicity was his passion,
Master of the playful sublime!

All morning I've been having fun
Imagining him in Baltimore,
Soused with crabmeat and National Bo,
Watching his very first game.

I can't wait till he finds out
About the infield fly rule.
He'll be beside himself with joy,
Beside me
                 there in the bleachers
As clouds like beautiful swimmers
Make their progress across the day.

Seated beneath tiers of sunlight
We'll watch something take place
He thought happened only in music,
Like his third splendid season
Arriving in perfect arabesques.

Outside time, we can sit in that
Heaven of baseball for as long

As he wants,
              rapt with continuity
And slow curves breaking,
Violin and violin echo,
Across the outside of the plate.

Walker Gibson
Umpire

♦

Everyone knows he's blind as a bat.
Besides, it's tricky to decide,
As ball meets mitt with a loud splat,
Whether it curved an inch outside
Or just an inch the other way
For a called strike. But anyway,
Nobody thinks that just because
Instead he calls that close one Ball,
That that was what it really *was*.
(The pitcher doesn't agree at all.)

His eyes are weak, his vision's blurred,
He can't tell a strike from a barn door —
And yet we have to take his word.
The pitch that was something else before
(And *there's* the mystery no one knows)
Has gotten to be a ball by now,
Or got to be called ball, anyhow.
All this explains why, I suppose,
People like to watch baseball games,
Where Things are not confused with Names.

Gary Gildner
4th Base

◆

Decked out in flannels and gripping my mitt
I was running laps, long grassy laps,
and hearing my 200 bones start to chatter —
I had finally arrived in the major leagues!

I stopped in the infield, dropping
to a shoulder stand — my big toes pointing out the sun! —
and there was no pain, even at 37.

Then we started to play — I was at 4th —
and my first throw over to 1st
bounced in on the 10th or 11th dribble.

Odd, I thought,
that the game had developed such wrinkles.
But shuck that, I was here now, bounding
around my sack like a well-oiled seal, barking
"Dust everyone off! Dust everyone off!"

After a while I slipped into Mass
and sat with my old teammates —
the ones from high school who had grown pink
and jowly, and who played with their keys
between their knees, and who
when the choir leaned forward to sing our song
covered their eyes, and mumbled, and wouldn't look at me.

In My Meanest Daydream

◆

I am throwing hard again
clipping corners, shaving
letters, dusting off
the heavy sticker crowding clean-up
clean down to his smelly socks —
& when my right spike hits
the ground he's had his look
already & gets
hollow in the belly —
in my meanest daydream I let fly
a sweet stream of spit, my catcher
pops his mitt
& grins
& calls me baby.

Speaking in Tongues

◆

In a light just right
for Boris Karloff's grin,
my guys are still too tight —
they throw like stiffs
the boogieman concocted out of
nuts and bolts and spider guts.
Balls are falling everywhere.
"George, I have a speech to make.
Tell these men the ball is
part of them, their arms, their souls —
it should travel true and beautiful.
They're moving like the devil's
got their peckers packed in ice."
He blushes. "Coach, that's complicated."
"OK, Georgie, tell them God
is hunkered on the bench behind us,
watching with His perfect squint,
a wad of Red Man bitter in His cheek.
Casey, Leo, Sparky, Yogi, John McGraw —
they're all around Him, close
but not too close: they hate it
when He dribbles chew across their cleats.
He hates it when a piece of soul is
muffed or thrown away.
Make it simple, Georgie. Listen:
God is hungry for a Warsaw win.
His stomach rumbles and He
mumbles to Himself, '. . . made a pocket
. . . made, like Michelangelo, two hands . . .
whenever both of these reach out
to help the pocket gobble up the ball
I am real glad . . .' "
In this frigid gym whose light's a cross

between Muscatel and hell, a shade
not even God can get the Polish
Boris Karloff bureaucrats to brighten,
George is talking turkey now,
passing on the word . . .
and my guys are trying hard to catch
the lingo and the rhythm.

Judy Goldman

Suicide

◆

The newspaper lied.
They did not find you
on the floor. Instead
you spent the afternoon
pitching with your son,
your face catching the silence
of the yard
like a soft leather glove
lovingly broken in.
And the light, the remarkable light,
ran over you so carelessly
it looked like silver numbers on your shirt.
You threw the ball for hours
as if there were no chance
night would ever search the corners
like the crowd
finding places in the stands,
their eyes marking the hard mound of dirt
below. For hours.
As if there were nothing at all
left to explain.

Donald Hall

Couplet

◆

Old Timers' Day, Fenway Park, 1 May 1982

When the tall puffy
figure wearing number
nine starts
late for the fly ball,
laboring forward
like a lame truckhorse
startled by a gartersnake,
— this old fellow
whose body we remember
as sleek and nervous
as a filly's —

and barely catches it
in his glove's
tip, we rise
and applaud weeping:
On a green field
we observe the ruin
of even the bravest
body, as Odysseus
wept to glimpse
among shades the shadow
of Achilles.

The Baseball Players

◆

Against the bright
grass the white-knickered
players tense, seize,
and attend. A moment
ago, outfielders
and infielders adjusted
their clothing, glanced
at the sun and settled
forward, hands on knees;
the catcher twitched
a forefinger; the pitcher
walked back of the hill,
established his cap
and returned; the batter
rotated his bat
in a slow circle.
                    But now
they pause: wary,
exact, suspended —
while abiding moonrise
lightens the angel
of the overgrown
garden, and Walter Blake
Adams, who died
at fourteen, waits
under the footbridge.

William Heyen

Mantle

◆

Mantle ran so hard, they said,
he tore his legs to pieces.
What is this but spirit?

52 homers in '56, the triple crown.
I was a high school junior, batting
fourth behind him in a dream.

I prayed for him to quit, before
his lifetime dropped below .300.
But he didn't, and it did.

He makes Brylcreem commercials now,
models with open mouths draped around him
as they never were in Commerce, Oklahoma,

where the sandy-haired, wide-shouldered boy
stood up against his barn,
lefty for an hour (Ruth, Gehrig),

then righty (DiMaggio),
as his father winged them in,
and the future blew toward him

now a fastball, now a slow
curve hanging
like a model's smile.

The Stadium

♦

The stadium is filled,
for this is the third night the moon
has not appeared as even a thin sickle.

We light the candles we were told to bring.
The diamond is lit red with torches.
Children run the bases.

A voice, as though from a tomb,
leads us to the last amen of a hymn.
Whole sections of the bleachers begin to moan.

The clergy files from the dugout
to the makeshift communion rails
that line the infield grass.

We've known, all our lives,
that we would gather here in the stadium
on just such a night,

that even the bravest among us
would weep softly in the dark aisles,
catching their difficult breath.

Conrad Hilberry

Instruction

◆

The coach has taught her how to swing,
run bases, slide, how to throw
to second, flip off her mask for fouls.

Now, on her own, she studies
how to knock the dirt out of her cleats,
hitch up her pants, miss her shoulder
with a stream of spit, bump
her fist into her catcher's mitt,
and stare incredulously at the ump.

Jonathan Holden

A Personal History of the Curveball

◆

It came to us like sex.
Years before we ever faced the thing
we'd heard about the curve
and studied it. Aerial photos
snapped by night in *Life*, mapping
Ewell "The Whip" Blackwell's sidearm hook,
made it look a fake, the dotted line
hardly swerved at all.
Such power had to be a gift
or else some trick, we didn't care which.
My hope was on technique.
In one mail-order course in hypnotism
that I took from the back cover
of a comic book, the hypnotist
like a ringmaster wore a suit,
sporting a black, Errol Flynn moustache
as he loomed, stern but benign
over a maiden.
Her eyes half-closed, she gazed
upward at his eyes, ready
to obey, as the zigzag lightning strokes
of his hypnotic power, emanating
from his fingertips and eyes,
passed into her stilled, receptive face.
She could feel
the tingling force-field of his powers.
After school, not knowing
what to look for, only
that we'd know it when it came —
that it would be strange —
we'd practice curves, trying
through trial and error to pick up by luck
whatever secret knack a curveball took,

sighting down the trajectory
of each pitch we caught
for signs of magic.
Those throws spun in like drills
and just as straight,
every one the same.
In Ebbets Field I'd watch
Sal "The Barber" Maglie train
his batter with a hard one at the head
for the next pitch,
some dirty sleight of hand down and away
he'd picked up somewhere
in the Mexican League. Done,
he'd trudge in from the mound.
His tired, mangy face had no illusions.
But the first curve I ever threw
that worked astonished me
as much as the lefty cleanup man I faced.
He dropped, and when I grinned
smiled weakly back. What he'd seen
I couldn't even guess
until one tepid evening in the Pony League
I stepped in against a southpaw,
a kid with catfish lips
and greased-back hair,
who had to be too stupid
to know any magic tricks. He lunged,
smote one at my neck.
I ducked. Then, either
that ball's spin broke every law
I'd ever heard about or else
Morris County moved almost
a foot. I was out
by the cheapest trick the air
can pull — Bernoulli's Principle.
Like "magic," the common love songs
wail and are eager to repeat
it helplessly, *magic*, as if to say
what else can I say, it's magic,
which is the stupidest of words
because it stands for nothing,

there is no magic. And yet
what other word does the heartbroken
or the strikeout victim have
to mean what cannot be and means what is?

Hitting Against Mike Cutler

◆

One down. I step into the narrow,
dust-floured shooting gallery, glance
out where the tall right-hander's squint
aims in to size things up. If it were up
to him, he'd take all afternoon he looks so
lazy — a gunslinger who just sauntered
into town, his jaw working over
a forgotten scrap of gum. He spits,
feels up the ball like a small, hard hornet;
and I hear the catcher settle in creaking
leather harness. He clucks contentedly,
does something dirty in his groin. Far
out there on the bright, bare, heat-rippling
hill the big guy nods. The hornet in his hand
begins to buzz. He bows. Slowly he
revolves away, then whirls, draws. I fire back.
The hornet hisses, vanishes with a BANG. STEE-RIKE!
The catcher grins. Good chuck, good chuck, he clucks.

How to Play Night Baseball

◆

A pasture is best, freshly
mown so that by the time a grounder's
plowed through all that chewed, spit-out
grass to reach you, the ball
will be bruised with green kisses. Start
in the evening. Come
with a bad sunburn and smelling of chlorine,
water still crackling in your ears.
Play until the ball is khaki —
a movable piece of the twilight —
the girls' bare arms in the bleachers are pale,
and heat lightning jumps in the west. Play
until you can only see pop-ups,
and routine grounders get lost in
the sweet grass for extra bases.

A Poem for Ed "Whitey" Ford

◆

I wanted my name
curt: Ed
Ford: a name that gave away
nothing. I wanted
a cute cocky face. To be
a low-ball specialist
but sneaky fast, tough
in the clutch. Not
to retire the side with power
but with finesse.
I never wanted to go
soft, to fall in love fall
through it and keep falling like this,
letting the light and air
pick my pockets at will.
Or dwell in this gray
area, this interval
where we search out by feel
the seams in the day,
homesick for the warm
map of a hand.
I planned to be
immune as Ford
on the throne of the mound,
my position defined
by both taut foul-lines,
the fence against my back.
To sight on the vanishing point
in the core of the mitt.
My delivery strict,
classic.
Not to sit thinking like this
how I drive the blunt wedge

of my breath before me
one space at a time,
watching words
I thought were well meant
miss. I wanted
what we all wanted then:
To be ice.
To throw uncontradicted
strikes. To be
like Ed Ford at work —
empty, cruel, accurate.
Our beauty pure expertise.

Richard Hugo
Letter to Mantsch from Havre

◆

Dear Mike: We didn't have a chance. Our starter had no change
and second base had not been plugged since early in July.
How this town turned out opening night of the tournament
to watch their Valley Furniture team wipe us, the No-
Name Tavern of Missoula, out. Remember Monty Holden,
ace Havre pitcher, barber, hero of the Highline, and his
tricky "catch-this" windup? First inning, when you hit that shot,
one on, the stands went stone. It still rockets the night.
I imagine it climbing today, somewhere in the universe,
lovelier than a girl climbs on a horse and lovelier than star.
We lost that game. No matter. Won another. Lost again
and went back talking fondly of your four home runs,
triple and single in three games, glowing in the record book.
I came back after poems. They ask me today, here in Havre,
who's that player you brought here years ago, the hitter?
So few of us are good at what we do, and what we do,
well done or not, seems futile. I'm trying to find Monty
Holden's barber shop. I want to tell him style in anything,
pitching, hitting, cutting hair, is worth our trying even
if we fail. And when that style, the graceful compact swing
leaves the home crowd hearing its blood and the ball roars off
in night like determined moon, it is our pleasure
to care about something well done. If he doesn't understand
more than the final score, if he says, "After all, we won,"
I'll know my hair will not look right after he's done,
what little hair I have, what little time. And I'll drive home
knowing his windup was all show, glad I was there years back,
that I was lucky enough to be there when with one swing
you said to all of us, this is how it's done. The ball jumps
from your bat over and over. I want my poems to jump
like that. All poems. I want to say once to a world that feels
with reason it has little chance, well done. That's the lie
I cannot shout loud as this local truth: Well done, Mike. Dick.

Missoula Softball Tournament

♦

This summer, most friends out of town
and no wind playing flash and dazzle
in the cottonwoods, music of the Clark Fork stale,
I've gone back to the old ways of defeat,
the softball field, familiar dust and thud,
pitcher winging drops and rises, and wives,
the beautiful wives in the stands, basic, used,
screeching runners home, infants unattended
in the dirt. A long triple sails into right center.
Two men on. Shouts from dugout: go, Ron, go.
Life is better run from. Distance to the fence,
both foul lines and dead center, is displayed.

I try to steal the tricky manager's signs.
Is hit-and-run the pulling of the ear?
The ump gives pitchers too much low inside.
Injustice? Fraud? Ancient problems focus
in the heat. Bad hop on routine grounder.
Close play missed by the team you want to win.
Players from the first game, high on beer,
ride players in the field. Their laughter
falls short of the wall. Under lights, the moths
are momentary stars, and wives, the beautiful wives
in the stands now take the interest they once feigned,
oh, long ago, their marriage just begun, years
of helping husbands feel important just begun,
the scrimping, the anger brought home evenings
from degrading jobs. This poem goes out to them.

Is steal-of-home the touching of the heart?
Last pitch. A soft fly. A can of corn
the players say. Routine, like mornings,
like the week. They shake hands on the mound.

Nice grab on that shot to left. Good game. Good game.
Dust rotates in their headlight beams.
The wives, the beautiful wives are with their men.

From Altitude, the Diamonds

◆

You can always spot them, even from high up,
the brown bulged out trying to make a circle
of a square, the green square inside the brown,
inside the green the brown circle you know is mound
and the big outside green rounded off by a round line
you know is fence. And no one playing.

You've played on every one. Second base somewhere
on the Dallas Tucson run, New Mexico you think,
where green was brown. Right field outside Chicago
where the fans went silent when you tripled home
the run that beat their best, their all-season
undefeated home town Sox. What a game you pitched
that hot day in the Bronx. You lost to that left hander,
Ford, who made it big, one-nothing on a fluke.
Who's to believe it now? Fat. Bald. Smoking your fear
of the turbulent air you are flying, remembering
the war, a worse fear, the jolting flak, the prayer.

When air settles, the white beneath you opens
and far below in some unpopulated region
of whatever state you are over (it can't be Idaho,
that was years ago) you spot a tiny diamond,
and because you've grown far sighted with age
you see players moving, the center fielder
running the ball down deep, two runners
rounding third, the third base coach waving hard
and the hitter on his own not slowing down
at second, his lungs filled with the cheers of those
he has loved forever, on his magnificent tiny way
to an easy stand-up three.

James Humphrey

The Athlete

◆

For Gwen Bell's and Catherine Thompson's
Junior and Senior English Students
Northeastern High School,
Elizabeth City, North Carolina,
May 26, 1987

I

Since I was 8, all I wanted in life
was to play centerfield for the St. Louis Cardinals.
Stepfather always punished me for doing well.
The better athlete I became, the worse the punishment.
He crippled me.
Ending it in near paralysis when I was 17.

Age 11, I was the only kid in the U.S.
who could drill the ball from the centerfield wall
in a professional park to the plate
on a single, perfect hop, nailing the runner.

That summer, I played midget and junior legion ball.
Some of the guys in legion
were 19 and 20. I started and batted third.
In midgets, I batted fourth. In both leagues,
we were state champions.

Next winter, I started left wing
for the high school hockey team.

First time I broad jumped, I leapt 19 feet 6 inches.
I was 12.
That same spring, I was the fastest 12 to 15-year-old
quarter-miler in the country, with a time of
53 seconds flat.

From age 8 to 12, I boxed in more than 100 fights
mostly against older boys, winning all the matches.

In gym at 16, I ran the mile once
— in tennis shoes
around the football field
in 4 minutes, 10 seconds,
probably a national record.
Nobody checked it out.
In full football gear, I punted the ball
50 yards, lofting it almost as high.

II

I became a poet
only when it was all that was left me,
except dying,
or giving into paralysis.

I didn't want to become a poet.
I should be wearing a world series
championship ring, be in the hall of fame,
doing color for ABC-TV's Monday Night
Baseball Game of the Week.

At 17, eight months before graduation,
stepfather made me quit highschool.

I lived in bushes and cardboard boxes.
Not expecting to last the winter,
I wrote my first poem A FALLEN MAN SEARCHING.
I wanted to define myself
before I starved or froze.

I believed, as I do now,
poems should shatter the surface of reality,
give us a new reality.

But poetry lived in the past, ignored innovation,
human motives, secrets of the heart,
honest emotion, human need,
rewarded those who obeyed its archaic rules,
continued the hollow ritual of snobbery.

III

I've endured 30 years in a literature
whose bosses
would rather have me out of the way.

I've tried to broaden poetry,
tried to bring it up-to-date
— make it a little ahead of its time
like music and art
— watching it remain the spoiled brat,
the least of literature.
30 years being ignored.

If we don't give it a human, contemporary voice
it will become, like Native Americans,
a lost tribe, confined to isolated areas
speaking entirely to itself.

Rolfe Humphries

Night Game

◆

Only bores are bored, —wrote William Saroyan —
And I was a bore, and so I went to the ball game;
But there was a pest who insisted on going with me.
I thought I could shake him if I bought one ticket,
But he must have come in on a pass. I couldn't see him,
But I knew he was there, back of third, in the row behind me,
His knees in my back, and his breath coming over my shoulder,
The loud-mouthed fool, the sickly nervous ego,
Repeating his silly questions, like a child
Or a girl at the first game ever. *Shut up*, I told him,
For Christ's sweet sake, shut up, and watch the ball game.
He didn't want to, but finally subsided,
And my attention found an outward focus,
Visible, pure, objective, inning by inning,
A well-played game, with no particular features, —
Feldman pitched well, and Ott hit a couple of homers.

And after the ninth, with the crowd in the bleachers thinning,
And the lights in the grandstand dimming out behind us,
And a full moon hung before us, over the clubhouse,
I drifted out with the crowd across the diamond,
Over the infield brown and smooth green outfield,
So wonderful underfoot, so right, so perfect,
That each of us was a player for a moment,
The men my age, and the soldiers and the sailors,
Their girls, and the running kids, and the plodding old men,
Taking it easy, the same unhurried tempo,
In the mellow light and air, in the mild cool weather,
Moving together, moving out together,
Oh, this is good, I felt, to be part of this movement,
This mood, this music, part of the human race,
Alike and different, after the game is over,
Streaming away to the exit, and underground.

[61]

Richard Jackson

Center Field

◆

I don't think it will ever come down,
it flew so quickly beyond the small hollow
the field lights make in the approaching dusk,
and I begin to realize how uneven the outfield is —
the small holes that test your ankles, the slight pitch
towards deep center that makes backpedaling so risky
but keeps pulling you as if further into your past.

It must be falling out of another world,
'lint from the stars' we used to say on a sandlot
in Lawrence, Mass. — and I have so much time
to imagine what you will say between innings
about what we try to steal from our darkening pasts,
how age means knowing how many steps we have lost,
remembering that too many friends have died,
and how love is the most important thing,
if only we knew who to love, and when.

The ball is just becoming visible again
and I am trying to remember anyone I have loved,
and it turns out it was usually too late, that we stood
like embarrassed batters caught looking at a third strike.
Yet somehow in this long moment I have slid
past the outstretched arms of twenty years,
and I can see Joey Gile crouched at third base
waiting, as it happened, for the bullet of some sniper
to snap like a line drive into his chest,
for John Kearns to swing and miss everything
from a tree in his back yard and not be found
for two days, for Joe Daly, whom I hardly knew
and who hardly had time to steal away
when the tractor slipped gear and tagged him to a tree,
for Gene Coskren who never understood baseball

and was fooled by a hit and run in Syracuse, N.Y.,
and somehow I am going to tell them all.

And my mother's sister who loved this game
and who complained for years about her stomach,
the family joke, until the cancer struck
and she went down faster than any of them.
And her own aunt, "I don't want to die," she said, and slid
her head to the pillow not out of fear
but embarrassment, stranded, she thought,
with no one to bring her home, no one to love.

But in the meantime, look, this is a poem
that could go on being about either death or love,
and we have only the uncertain hang time
of a fly ball to decide how to position ourselves,
to find the right words for our love,
to turn towards home as the night falls, as the ball,
as the loves, the deaths we grab for our own.

Don Johnson

Home Game

◆

Heat lightning silhouettes the hills
beyond the worn-out pasture
where I lob slow pitches toward a flat rock
that no longer gleams like the white rubber plate
of the majors. My father taps soft liners

to my son. Professionally crouched
over burdocks, poised above the looped runners
of morning glories, the boy breaks
with each ring of the new metal bat, stumbles
through sedge and almost catches everything.

Wearing my tattered glove like a badge,
he dreams fences for the open field,
rags the old man to hit the long ball
he could climb the wall for like Yastrzemski.
He is out there where I have been

in the child's sweatless world of fame,
but I would have changed that thunder
building on the river to the first murmur
of applause that lived already as a faint twitch
troubling the sleep of boys throughout Virginia.

My father stole every sign and took my dream
to manage, ran it as he ran me in this very field
at dusk behind his tractor, crying "push, push, push,"
when I let up. In the listening air
his voice seemed to fade toward the waiting house,

to blend with my mother's calling us in
to supper. Now with clouds coming on
like middle age I want to tell my son

that dreams cost more than years,
that a bush league curve will earn

a lifetime's worth of nights in damp motels.
But I wave him back against a stand of pines
and turn in the rain's first spattering
to face my father, still crowding the plate
at sixty. The old game again. He knows

I mean to blow three quick ones by him, win
finally, before the night and the storm's dark
tarpaulin sweep in from deepest center field.
With the boy watching like a deer
from the tree line, I get two strikes clean,

then thunder booms overhead, the sound
of a high hard one splintering barn board
at my ear, bringing back his fatherly words:
"It's all in the delivery,
knowing when to bear down."

On the porch the women wave their white arms,
my mother, my wife, his wife, the boy's mother,
still calling us in as I wind up,
float the fat one down the middle, hearing
the ball peal off the level swing as I whirl

to track the high arc toward the clouds.
My son fades into pine boughs, bent on glory.
I stand here, face masked in rain, knowing
the old man stands at my back, his silver Adirondack
stuck into the storm, daring the lightning down.

And the River Gathered
around Us

◆

After they wheeled away the town,
when the floodgates closed
and the river turned on itself,
we came back day after day
to watch the coves slowly fill up.

At the end of a week one road in
lay open. We drove it in three
Ford cars and a pickup towing
Wash Holt's rubber-tired wagon
that the boys from Mountain City rode.

It was not a Sunday. Most of us
had jobs, but we agreed to one more
game of ball before the smoothest
diamond in three counties
turned to lake bottom.

Water already lapped at the right field
fence where I killed a snake
before the first pitch, a fast ball
the batter himself called
a strike since we had no umpire.

Right went under with two out
in their half of the third
and we declared a ground ball
to that field an out. I played
barefoot and cheated toward

the infield, but it didn't matter.
Before the fifth was over,
water covered all but the mound

and the raked dirt at the plate.
By then, anything not a bunt

or fly ball was an out
and we were losing 6–2
when their pitcher called time
and said all three balls we had
were water-logged and that

he wouldn't ruin his arm
for no damn game in a lake,
so we brought him in half-way
where it was wet but close enough
to lob those melons in

with no pain. Then we lost
the bases, but ruled that running
in the right direction counted
if the runner didn't stop
until he made it home

or got out. We tied the score
on four straight hits to left
when a jon boat floated through
and blocked the fielder's way.
We called anything that hit

the boat a homer and it rained
that inning, the score tied
and water finally touching
the plate where both teams
congregated, soaked and up

to our knees in a field
without bounds, where everything
slowed and floated and nothing
sliding beneath the flood
would ever be forgotten.

Halvard Johnson

Americans Playing
Slow-Pitch Softball at an
Airbase near Kunsan,
South Korea

◆

— Early September

The first game of
the evening begins
about five-thirty.

The men (not that
only men play —
one team has

a female catcher)
finish their work
on whatever they

work on —
correspondence,
water mains, Phantoms —

get out of one uniform,
into another, and come
out to the ballpark.

The lights go on early.
By eight here it's totally
dark. Half an hour earlier

the sky was a tangle
of rose, magenta,
lavender, as the sun

went down in China,
beyond the Yellow Sea.
Brisk wind tonight —

raises the infield dirt,
whips it into narrowed eyes
of batter, catcher, umpire,

the three or four spectators
in the bleachers behind them.
A regulation seven-inning

game is played, unless one
team is so far out in front
that the ten-run rule

is invoked, ending
the game after five. A ball
the size of a small

grapefruit is lofted
into the air, a slight
backspin making it

seem to drift and float
down toward the plate.
No easy hit. The batter

has to apply his own
muscle to put it anywhere.
This batsman clips the top

and bounces to the third
baseman, who fires to first
for an easy out. He shrugs

and jogs to the dugout.
The next batter flies out,
and the game ends 15-zip

after five full innings.
Another two teams take the field.
Some of the players stand

[69]

by to watch the second game,
but most wander off,
concerned with other things.

The bleachers are fuller now —
a rowdier crowd, raring for action.
Crisp evening air. Korean girlfriends

cuddle close for warmth. An airman
pops open a beer. Behind their
backs a pair of Phantoms

roar into the sky, their afterburners
glowing as they lift from the runway,
vanish into black clouds. Uncertain

weather tonight, a stiff wind, high
scudding clouds. A tricky weather
system reaching north to

the DMZ, east to the Sea of Japan,
south to the East China Sea.
Typhoon Orchid approaches Okinawa,

far to the southeast. Possibly
this is all a part of that. Inning
after inning goes by, vanishing

into a past that exists only on paper.
Hits, runs, and errors go down
in the league's record book,

but screw the past, we're having
fun tonight. Neither the pitcher,
the fliers, nor the Korean

women in the stands
remember or care about a war
that happened thirty years ago.

It's the girls' fathers who have
the bad dreams, wake in terror in
the night. Their grandfathers, too.

They'll all support General Chun
and pray he'll protect them
from devils. A friend of mine

in Europe once wrote a poem
about memory and the historical
imagination, which ended

with these lines:
"Our assignment is to remember,
to deliver blows."

No American could have written that.
We live our lives inning by inning,
season by season, war by war.

I'll end this in an American way —
with the words of the great black,
American pitcher, Satchel Paige:

> "Don't look back.
> Something may be
> gaining on you."

Laurence Lieberman
My Father Dreams of Baseball

◆

On hot September nights, when sleep is scarce,
in place of sheep Dad counts home runs that carry
the left-field fence and fly clean out of the ball park.

      Father snaps off the twi-night doubleheader;
      Behind his back, the screen door loosens a hinge.
      He escapes to the backyard retreat to rant at the ump.
      Hopped-up in the Porsche, he's off for an all-night binge.

      By morning, Mother's throat has a telltale lump.
      He takes his losses hard, a heavy bettor.

In his dreams, white dashing figures circle the bases.
Their caps dazzle in the sun like lights on a scoreboard.
The diamond is worn a foot deep under hammering cleats.

      He attends home games. Through Dad's binoculars
      the power hitters charge home plate like bulls,
      and make the picador pitcher's heart stand still.
      (A curve ball is a lance that bull's-eyes skulls.)
      My father in the stands directs the kill
      like a black matador in Madrid spectaculars.

Just inches inside the foul line, a figure is poised
three feet in the air, his arm outstretched for the catch.
His mouth is pinched with the pain of a near-miss.
The features are fixed with the dull metallic glow
of an ancient face, cast in bronze or brass.

Carol Masters

Fly Ball

◆

A fly ball
has nothing of flight about it
it's pushed out there
its trajectory absolute
as the slap of the bat

but no one has ever seen
a ball go into the glove
it's true
follow the arc
unblinking the slow climb up the last leg
of the mountain   the raising of a flag   salute
the sure sail home to the cup
of the mitt

suddenly the field breaks up
everyone running the same way
a terrible accident
Christ has landed
at International Airport
your presence is required

no it's just the game   over
you missed it
in that last inch
the ball disappears

in fact there's a moment when the ball never enters the glove
it decides to cock a wing
veer to the south
    so long folks   I'm off on a jet-
    stream that sweet south
    wind in my wingpits   we're all going

all U.S. fly balls going to take off
like popcorn roll down the coast
and bloom like migratory monarchs
on the trees of Argentina

no it's still coming
a single headlight   you below it
on the tracks

the ball ballooning
rides clear as an onion
breaking from its skin
that terrible moon

coming
damn thing never stops
blazing with possibilities
and it's yours   you claim it
whether you want it or not
it will come   what matters
is where you are

William Matthews

The Hummer

◆

First he drew a strike zone
on the toolshed door, and then
he battered against it all summer
a balding tennis ball, wetted
in a puddle he tended under
an outdoor faucet: that way
he could see, at first, exactly
where each pitch struck.
Late in the game the door
was solidly blotched and
calling the corners was fierce
enough moral work for any
man he might grow up to be.
His stark rules made it hard
to win, and made him finish
any game he started, no matter
if he'd lost it early.
Some days he pitched
six games, the last in dusk,
in tears, in rage, in the blue
blackening joy of obsession.
If he could have been also
the batter, he would have been,
trying to stay alive. Twenty-
seven deaths a game and all
of them his. For a real game
the time it takes is listed
in the box score, the obituary.
What he loved was mowing
them down. Thwap. Thwap.
Then one thwap low and outside.
And finally the hummer.
It made him grunt to throw it,
as if he'd tried to hold it
back, but it escaped. Thwap.

Gail Mazur

Baseball

◆

The game of baseball is not a metaphor
and I know it's not really life.
The chalky green diamond, the lovely
dusty brown lanes I see from airplanes
multiplying around the cities
are only neat playing fields.
Their structure is not the frame
of history carved out of forest,
that is not what I see on my ascent.

And down in the stadium,
the veteran catcher guiding the young
pitcher through the innings, the line
of concentration between them,
that delicate filament is not
like the way you are helping me,
only it reminds me when I strain
for analogies, the way a rookie strains
for perfection, and the veteran,
in his wisdom, seems to promise it,
it glows from his upheld glove,

and the man in front of me
in the grandstand, drinking banana
daiquiris from a thermos,
continuing through a whole dinner
to the aromatic cigar even as our team
is shut out, nearly hitless, he is
not like the farmer that Auden speaks
of in Breughel's Icarus,
or the four inevitable woman-hating
drunkards, yelling, hugging
each other, and moving up and down
continuously for more beer

and the young wife trying to understand
what a full count could be
to please her husband happy in
his old dreams, or the little boy
in the Yankees cap already nodding
off to sleep against his father,
program and popcorn memories
sliding into the future,
and the old woman from Lincoln, Maine,
screaming at the Yankee slugger
with wounded knees to break his leg

this is not a microcosm,
not even a slice of life
and the terrible slumps,
when the greatest hitter mysteriously
goes hitless for weeks, or
the pitcher's stuff is all junk
who threw like a magician all last month,
or the days when our guys look
like Sennett cops, slipping, bumping
each other, then suddenly, the play
that wasn't humanly possible, the Kid
we know isn't ready for the big leagues,
leaps into the air to catch a ball
that should have gone downtown,
and coming off the field is hugged
and bottom-slapped by the sudden
sorcerers, the winning team

the question of what makes a man
slump when his form, his eye,
his power aren't to blame, this isn't
like the bad luck that hounds us,
and his frustration in the games
not like our deep rage
for disappointing ourselves

the ball park is an artifact,
manicured, safe, "scene in an Easter egg,"
and the order of the ball game,
the firm structure with the mystery

of accidents always contained,
not the wild field we wander in,
where I'm trying to recite the rules,
to repeat the statistics of the game,
and the wind keeps carrying my words away

The Idea of Florida
during a Winter Thaw

◆

Late February and the air's so balmy
snowdrops and crocuses may be fooled
into early blooming. Then, the inevitable blizzard
will come, blighting our harbingers of spring,
and the glum yards will go back undercover.
Odd to think that in Florida it's strawberry
season — shortcake, waffles, berries and cream
will soon be pencilled on the coffeeshop menus.

In Winter Haven, the ballplayers are stretching
and preening, dancing on the basepaths,
giddy as good kids playing hookey. Now,
for a few weeks, statistics won't seem
to matter, for the flushed boys are muscular
and chaste, lovely as lakes to the retired men
watching calisthenics from the grandstands.
Escapees from the cold work of living,

the old men burnish stories of Yaz and the Babe
and the Splendid Splinter. For a few dreamy dollars,
they sit with their wives all day in the sun,
on their own little seat cushions, wearing soft caps
with visors. Their brave recreational vehicles
grow hot in the parking lot, though they're
shaded by liveoaks and bottlebrush trees
whose soft bristles graze the top-racks.

At four, the spectators leave in pairs, off
to restaurants for Early Bird Specials.
A salamander scuttles across the quiet
visitors' dugout. The osprey whose nest is atop
the foul pole relaxes. She's raged all afternoon
at balls hit again and again toward her offspring.

Although December's frost killed the winter crop,
there's a pulpy orange-y smell from juice factories. . . .

Down the road, at Cypress Gardens, a woman
trainer flips young alligators over on their backs,
demonstrating their talent for comedy — stroke
their bellies and they're out cold, instantaneously
snoozing. A schoolgirl on vacation gapes,
wonder if she'd ever be brave enough
to try that, to hold a terrifying beast
and turn it into something cartoon-funny.

She stretches a hand toward the toothy sleeper
then takes a step back, to be safe as she reaches.

Linda Mizejewski

Season Wish

◆

In turns of season
come exchanges,
transformations — daughters, even,
traded to gods for wheat or rain.
Rapunzel, before she was even born,
was traded away for cabbage leaves
on a risk her father took one night
for love. A man might think of dowry
on a night that pivots warmth and cold
during Indian summers, false
springs, sudden August cool.
A miller might say his daughter
can spin horses' straw to gold.
A man might offer in sudden hope
a crop, a dove, his youngest girl.

In spring, my father
took me out at dusk
to lots the boys had left,
seeing each year if I could spin
the winning curve ball back to him
and learn to catch, the grip and swing
of a missing son; hoping there was magic
in the glove or sneakers or wooden bat
like the power children found
in the legend in pauper's clothes
that created a man from balls of snow.
The cap, perhaps, might keep my hair
forever clipped; holding the glove
against my chest might stop
my breasts; and if I learned
the grip and stance, perhaps my wrists
would thicken, hard, around the bat.

My father made the diamond
out of stones he piled like altars
into three small mounds.
Pitching to him underhand,
sometimes I threw him winning runs
and watched him round our bases,
touch the stones and then
take home. He hoped
the season would never come
when something more important
would keep me on an April night
from trespassing with him into lots
till boys came back
to claim their ground
and kick our home and bases
into rocks again.

Year by year he built for me
the things he thought
a man one day would want me for:
investments, a name
the family business — stock
to insure a fair exchange
for a man who might try
to be a son. My father's
spring trades always failed:
I always came back being
still a girl who couldn't play
the way he'd hoped while he
built for me stone bases
on his knees there in the dirt.

Larry Moffi
Comparative Theology
◆

He is a lesson in theology,
my neighbor, a fan of the Cubs
the children on the block, cruel
and mis-understanding call Count Dracula
because they think he loves the dark
when, truly, it is everything unnatural
in electricity he abhors. I might
explain how good that impulse is,
and what it means to hold daylight
sacred, in which all that is good
grows and gives back of itself
freely and green. But I have heard him
summer evenings after work, evangelical
in the garden, another lost tribe,
a congregation of one condemned
to repeat history, orally, and off-key
singing of the long and difficult shadows
and the late inning rallies, of next
year in the land of the midnight sun.
It is our private sufferings made public
that separate us in faith.

Lillian Morrison

When I Was a Kid

◆

I played outfield
in the stickball games
on the cobblestone sidestreets
of Jersey City, N.J.
Made some good catches,
jumping grabs, beautiful onehanders
up on the far-off sidewalks
as I crashed against fences.

My fan club of one,
old Mr. Graham, retired fireman,
white mustaches glowing, red
face growing ruddier between
nips from a wine bottle, sat
on his stoop's top step every
afternoon, shaking his head,
gloating at each neat snaring,
each throw on a line to home plate.
"What a girl, what a wing," he'd say.

Now out at the edge of the mind
I try not to let the apt words,
the soaring images slip through
my brain fingers; I want to trap
them, throw them into the action
on all the wings I can muster
but I miss a good many and when I
glance at the sidelines, — no,
no smiling white mustaches,
no happy red face.

Of Kings and Things

♦

What happened to Joey on our block
Who could hit a spaldeen four sewers
And wore his invisible crown
With easy grace, leaning, body-haloed
In the street-lamp night?

He was better than Babe Ruth
Because we could actually see him hit
Every Saturday morning,
With a mop handle thinner than any baseball bat,
That small ball which flew forever.
Whack! straight out at first, then
Rising, rising unbelievably soaring in a
Tremendous heart-bursting trajectory
To come down finally, blocks away,
Bouncing off a parked car's
Fender, eluding the lone outfielder.

Did he get a good job?
Is he married now, with kids?
Is he famous in another constellation?
I saw him with my own eyes in those days
The God of stickball
Disappearing down the street
Skinny and shining in the nightfall light.

Tim Peeler

Curt Flood

◆

try to tell 'em Curt,
how you crowned their wallets,
climbed courtroom steps
for them,
swallowed that black ball,
a scapegoat out to pasture.
they don't remember,
can't remember
the trash you ate,
your greedy headlines,
the slope of your career.

you are a ghost at barterer's wing,
your smokey gray eyes
are two extra zeroes
on every contract.

Donald Petersen

The Ballad of Dead Yankees

◆

Where's Babe Ruth, the King of Swat,
Who rocked the heavens with his blows?
Grabowski, Pennock, and Malone —
Mother of mercy, where are those?

Where's Tony (Poosh 'em up) Lazzeri,
The quickest man that ever played?
Where's the gang that raised the roof
In the house that Colonel Ruppert made?

Where's Lou Gehrig, strong and shy,
Who never missed a single game?
Where's Tiny Bonham, where's Jake Powell
And many another peerless name?

Where's Steve Sundra, good but late,
Who for a season had his fling?
Where are the traded, faded ones?
Lord, can they tell us anything?

Where's the withered nameless dwarf
Who sold us pencils at the gate?
Hurled past the clamor of our cheers?
Gone to rest with the good and great?

Where's the swagger, where's the strut,
Where's the style that was the hitter?
Where's the pitcher's swanlike motion?
What in God's name turned life bitter?

For strong-armed Steve, who lost control
And weighed no more than eighty pounds,
No sooner benched than in his grave,
Where's the cleverness that confounds?

For Lou the man, erect and clean,
Wracked with a cruel paralysis,
Gone in his thirty-seventh year,
Where's the virtue that was his?

For nimble Tony, cramped in death,
God knows why and God knows how,
Shut in a dark and silent house,
Where's the squirrel quickness now?

For big brash Babe in an outsize suit,
Himself grown thin and hoarse with cancer,
Still autographing balls for boys,
Mother of mercy, what's the answer?

Is there a heaven with rainbow flags,
Silver trophies hung on walls,
A horseshoe grandstand, mobs of fans,
Webbed gloves and official balls?

Is there a power in judgment there
To stand behind the body's laws,
A stern-faced czar whose slightest word
Is righteous as Judge Kenesaw's?

And if there be no turnstile gate
At that green park, can we get in?
Is the game suspended or postponed,
And do the players play to win?

Mother of mercy, if you're there,
Pray to the high celestial czar
For all of these, the early dead,
Who've gone where no ovations are.

Jack Ridl
Good Training for Poetry

◆

"Thanks," my father said, and slapped
my right hand as I rounded
third. I'd hit the first
pitch of my first at bat in college
high across an April sky and onto
the highway behind the scoreboard
in right center, the only
home run I would ever hit.
It kept me at second
till my senior year, when suddenly
I lost my eye,
couldn't hit a cantaloupe
with a tennis racquet,
and took my place
next to the freshmen,
watched the season go by
like a hit batsman trotting to first,
shaking off the sting.
Now, one week each spring
I watch my daughter
take her cuts, slap her hand
into the pocket of her mitt.
And now my father
steadies his eye,
lining up his daily round
of twelve foot putts. He sinks
five out of seven. I still
feel his hand, still
wonder why I ended
like a blind man
on the bench, a daughter
dashing home from first,
a father dropping out of sight.

Mike Shannon

The Art of Baseball Poetry

◆

A baseball poem should be high and tight
As a fastball on a hitter's night,

Sharp
As a line drive off the tarp,

Lazy as a high fly ball
Fungoed to a pitcher near the wall —

A baseball poem should be artless
As a rookie's heart.

❀   ❀   ❀   ❀

Ball poems should be tossed around
Before returning to the mound,

Felt, and scuffed, and squeezed
Until the proper grip is found,

And caught in the pocket, if you please,
To furnish the diamond that old popping sound,

Ball poems should be tossed around
Before returning to the mound.

❀   ❀   ❀   ❀

A baseball poem should be yellow at night:
Not trite.

For year-round lifelong love
The broken laces of a fielder's glove.

For joy
Calisthenics in the Arizona sun and a bird dog in the bushes.

A baseball poem should be
Poetry.

Tom Sheehan

In Cold Fields

◆

They left us then,
we in our sneakers
and innocence
of those bright summer days,
to go away from us
with our big brothers,
left us lonely and miserable
on corners, in cold fields
with all the long-ball hitters gone,
the big sticks of the neighborhood,
and the big wood of the Majors,
and we cried in dark cells of home
for our brothers and bubble-gum heroes,
a community of family.

Oh, Eddie's brother not yet home
from someplace in World War II,
Zeke's brother who owned the soul
of every pitcher he ever caught,
a shortstop the Cards owned,
Spillane, I think, his name;
and in that great silence out there
Billy centerfield left his arm
in Kwajalein debris.

Oh, brotherless we played our game,
no deep outfield, no zing to pitch,
no speed, no power, loveless
without a big brother
to show the growing.

And then, not long after the Braves
rode that mighty crest,

our turn came,
and we left our brothers
on corners, in cold fields,
we long-ball hitters.

Arthur Smith

Extra Innings

♦

Back then the ballpark grass was so overgrown
      and sweet-smelling, I think
I could have bellied down near the dugout
And drowsed away the afternoon. He was, then, simply

Someone on the mound. I went one-for-three —
The single, along with a strikeout and a towering pop-up
      that was, as one wit quipped,
A home run in an elevator shaft. Four months later

He was called up by the Mets. The rest, as we say,
      is history. We say a lot
Of stupid things. We know our bodies are not luminous
      like the stars,
And so we make amends: we think ourselves luminous
      the moment

Sleep comes on, or after loving someone loved —
      that warmth
Radiating out like sound, a name called and carried off
      on the air — or,
Better, and far richer, because it happened once,
      after breaking up

A no-hitter by Tom Seaver, with two out in the ninth.
That was almost twenty years ago, and here I am again
      rounding first, braking,
The dust whirled into a flurry at my feet and the relay
      coming back in

To the pitcher, who has turned away, his face now blurred
      beyond recognition.

Whoever he is, Seaver, or someone nameless like myself —
    a landscaper, perhaps,
As good as any other, catching his breath under an ash tree
    on a new-mown lawn — if he remembers anything,

He'll remember the sun flowing the length of his arm
    before flaring out
Into a slider no one could touch all afternoon.
He'll remember his no-hitter as precisely

And firmly as I remember spoiling it, and neither of us
    is wrong. Seaver has his stats,
And the rest of us are stuck with rearranging, cutting
And mixing, working day and night, in dreams, in the dark
    of a warehouse

Stacked with the daily, disintegrating rushes of 20 and 30
    and 40 years ago,
Trying to make it right, remixing, trying to accommodate
    what happened with what
Might have happened. And it never turns out true,

The possibilities not to be trusted but, rather,
Believed in against the facts — whatever they are:
    the low liner hanging
Long enough for the left fielder to dive for, tumbling,

And the graceful pop-up
To his feet, the ball visible, clearly,
In the webbing of the glove held

High over his head, the third out, the proof
That this, ah, yes, this is what happened, the fans in
    his memory standing,
Roaring in disbelief, and the lovely applause lasting
    till he's off the field.

Dave Smith

For Willie Still in Center

◆

The walls of Southern pine or Northern brick
still stand where you crumpled or just stopped
short of the smashed jaw and the gut rip. They
dog us to our dugouts like the expected thing
that didn't happen. All these years so easily

you've turned, twisted, whipped the impossible
shot home, then nonchalantly trotted in to knock
our children back into their rude country dreams.
Even the Birmingham Bombers could do nothing to
change you: you were born to straddle center.

But Time is always a rookie forcing the walls
to move back, forcing owners to expand the green
aisles where the legs do not often stumble and snap,
forcing players to take up the options of men.
Yet your eyes are still fiery and tight as those

of children who sleep and wake running with backs
to the man with the stick, hustling like hell to
get where you are: that glorious circle of light
dead in center with the ancient faces of Bombers
patting you on the back like any hometown hero.

You are their myth, uncommitted until the last
crack of the bat, still on your toes and taking
hung curves in stride as you sweep into and out
of the white lights, and not one has told you
their children are not on their toes, whose cleats
dig in like bombs, whose eyes are something to see.

Mean Rufus Throw Down

◆

He waits perpetually crouched, teeth,
tongue, raw knuckles, tattooed muscles
bunched under his hide like clouds,
taking and taking and taking until
the right moment tears his eyes open,
his arm, like a lover's curse, snakes
swiftly out to second eating the silky
air of the proudest runner, ending the game.

The Roundhouse Voices

◆

In full glare of sunlight I came here, man-tall but thin
as a pinstripe, and stood outside the rusted fence
with its crown of iron thorns while
the soot cut into our lungs with tiny diamonds.
I walked through houses with my grain-lovely slugger
from Louisville that my uncle bought and stood
in the sun that made its glove soft on my hand
until I saw my chance to crawl under and get past
anyone who would demand a badge and a name.

The guard hollered that I could get the hell from there quick
when I popped in his face like a thief. All I ever wanted
to steal was life and you can't get that easy
in the grind of a railyard. *You can't catch me,
lardass, I can go left or right good as the Mick,*
I hummed to him, holding my slugger by the neck
for a bunt laid smooth where the coal cars
jerked and let me pass between tracks
until, in a slide on ash, I fell safe and heard
the wheeze of his words: *Who the hell are you, kid?*

I hear them again tonight, Uncle, hard as big brakeshoes,
when I lean over your face in the box of silk. The years
you spent hobbling from room to room alone crawl
up my legs and turn this house to another
house, round and black as defeat, where slugging
comes easy when you whip the gray softball over
the glass diesel globe. Footsteps thump on the stairs
like that fat ball against bricks and when I miss
I hear you warn me to watch the timing, to keep
my eyes on your hand and forget the fence,

hearing also that other voice that keeps me out and away
from you on a day worth playing good ball. Hearing
Who the hell . . . I see myself like a burning speck
of cinder come down the hill and through a tunnel
of porches like stands, running on deep ash,
and I give him the finger, whose face still gleams
clear as a B&O headlight, just to make him get up
and chase me into a dream of scoring at your feet.
At Christmas that guard staggered home sobbing,
the thing in his chest tight as a torque wrench.
In the summer I did not have to run and now

who is the one who dreams of a drink as he leans over
tools you kept bright as a first-girl's promise? I
have no one to run from or to, nobody to give
my finger to as I steal his peace. Uncle, the light
bleeds on your gray face like the high barbed-wire
shadows I had to get through and maybe you don't remember
you said to come back, to wait and you'd show me
the right way to take a hard pitch
in the sun that shudders on the ready man. I'm here

though this is a day I did not want to see. In the roundhouse
the rasp and heel-click of compressors is still,
soot lies deep in every greasy fingerprint.
I called you from the pits and you did not come up
and I felt the fear when I stood on the tracks
that are like stars which never lead us
into any kind of light and I don't know who'll
tell me now when the guard sticks his blind snoot
between us: take off and beat the bastard out.
Can you hear him over the yard, grabbing his chest,
cry out, *Who the goddamn hell are you, kid?*

I gave him every name in the book, Uncle, but he caught us
and what good did all those hours of coaching do?
You lie on your back, eyeless forever, and I think
how once I climbed to the top of a diesel and stared
into that gray roundhouse glass where, in anger,
you threw up the ball and made a star
to swear at greater than the Mick ever dreamed.

It has been years but now I know what followed there
every morning the sun came up, not light
but the puffing bad-bellied light of words.

All day I have held your hand, trying to say back that life,
to get under that fence with words I lined
and linked up and steamed into a cold room
where the illusion of hope means skin torn in boxes
of tools. The footsteps come pounding into words
and even the finger I give death is words
that won't let us be what we wanted, each one
chasing and being chased by dreams in the dark.
Words are all we ever were and they did us
no damn good. Do you hear that?

Do you hear the words that, in oiled gravel, you gave me
when you set my feet in the right stance to swing?
They are coal-hard and they come in wings
and loops like despair not even the Mick
could knock out of this room, words softer
than the centers of hearts in guards or uncles,
words skinned and numbed by too many bricks.
I have had enough of them and bring them back here
where the tick and creak of everything dies
in your tiny starlight and I stand down
on my knees to cry, *Who the hell are you, kid?*

R. T. Smith
Softball at Julia Tutwiler Prison

◆

The pitcher shot her husband
and more than one felon
chatters zealously in the infield.
I come here once a month
with a busload of Episcopalians
to engage the women prisoners
on the dirt diamond of their yard.

They beat us every time,
depending on the hot arm
of a black girl from Wetumpka,
the dangerous base runners
and our reliable errors.
They have mastered this space.

Any shot knocked over the fence,
either fair or foul,
is a ground rules home run here.
Wardens always umpire,
fudging a bit for the visitors.
Irony is in the air.

In today's late innings
their shortstop has converted
to plug up our infield hole,
just to make things interesting.
They become generous
with the strange taste of winning.

In the makeshift dugout we share
talk runs from gothic novels
to Thanksgiving dinner.
Not a soul mentions escape
or athletic fellowship.

Now with two easy outs gone
in the ninth, I step up to bat,
eye the left field fence,
a smiling girl on the mound.
I have not hit safely all day,
but I want to change it all.

The ball is spinning slow motion.
I swing with every muscle
toward the fallen sun, swing
for guilt and the electric fence,
swing like hell for all of us.

Ron Smith

Striking Out My Son
in the Father-Son Game

◆

Caught in the open in broad daylight,
jerky-eyed with doubt,
he swings like someone
who's never held a bat.

His elbows wrongly angle in,
his wrists are snapless
when the soft, lopsided sphere
drops from the sky.

Anyway, those wobbly ankles
and rattly knees cannot
spank those Nikes off the bases
or make a proper feet-first slide.

His eyes are everywhere
but on the ball. I arc
three adequate pitches
and retire the side.

We joke our stiff adult jokes
to the plate and cock
our clubs at our squawking,
crouching sons.

Despite the jolt to dozing muscles,
we find we can still hit
and run. Bellies leaning
toward the outfield,

we circle and circle the bags.
On the mound a grim boy tiptoes
to see his best pitch ride
into the left field pines.

Another banker scores.
My son slinks among a dozen fielders,
trying to hide.
He will have to come

to the plate again
with that gap between his fists
I haven't made him close.
I climb the red clay,

toe the rubber, and spit.
From a row of hooting women
my wife glares at me
through the shimmer of heat.

She can see the blood in my face
that means the steeper drop,
the slow backspin. These little boys
will never hit me today.

Dabney Stuart

Swinging on the First Pitch

◆

You go up there cocked.
You don't care if the whole
stadium knows you're hitting away.
After all, he's been bringing
the first one in from the start.
There's no need to look
it over. It's the same stuff
you've been taking all day, all
season, since you can remember.
So what if the two of you keep
leading the league in strikeouts,
at least this time he's not getting
ahead of you while you stand there
taking up space. Anybody
can do that, that's what other people
buy tickets for.
If he doesn't groove it, you're sure
it'll be in the strike zone,
or near, and the way you feel
it could be a mile off and you'd still
go with it, dump it down the line
for a double. You're ready
for anything he's got, dug in, rippling
the air, wrists rolling smooth
in the box ready
for anything.
He goes into his motion —
the same old cunnythumb herkyjerk
sidesaddle nonsense, nothing
up his sleeve but what you've known
is there all along — winds,
delivers. It's a fast ball,
big as a globe, 110
miles an hour, coming
right at your head.

[105]

Full Count

♦

Reality is what the rest of life is about.
— TV baseball documentary

The umpire's blind
and the pitcher's throwing tin cups.
They waver and dip,
sail and teeter, not one of them
coming straight and true
or curving predictably.
A knuckle ball would be
a Godsend.
It's like believing
stories about the world
are the world.
I foul everything off,
a piece here, a tic there.
The catcher finally curls
up for a nap at the umpire's feet.
The umpire thinks
it's his dog; he assumes
the game's over and he's back
on his porch in his rocking chair.
He lights his pipe,
tilts, releases.
Once upon a time he says.
The benches empty
but no one argues.
His word is indisputable.
Players mill and joke,
the managers shake hands and spit.
The pitcher and I dip cool water
from a bucket, drink
from the cup between us.
The crowd drifts onto the grass,
sits amiably. They toss
their rain checks aside;

a breeze lifts them into the bright air
like confetti at a parade,
like balloons rising,
like the umpire's words.
His story goes on
past suppertime, past the arclights'
eventual sudden
blaze into the dark.
No one tires, or tries
to predict what happens next.
After mornings of unbearable
loveliness, after the water
and tobacco run out —
whenever the end comes —
we will still be here, settled
into the voice of our calling.

James Tate

The Buddhists Have the Ball Field

◆

The Buddhists have the ball field. Then the teams
arrive, nine on one, but only three on the other.
The teams confront the Buddhists. The Buddhists
present their permit. There is little point in
arguing it, for the Buddhists clearly have the
permit for the field. And the teams have nothing,
not even two complete teams. It occurs to one team
manager to interest the Buddhists in joining his
team, but the Buddhists won't hear of it. The teams
walk away with their heads hung low. A gentle rain
begins. It would have been called anyway, they
think suddenly.

Rodney Torreson

Two Years Retired, Bobby Murcer Makes a Comeback Bid, 1985

◆

The life of a soul on earth lasts longer than his departure.

— Outfielder Murcer
quoting philosopher-poet Angelo Patri
at Thurman Munson's funeral, 1979

After your ascent into the
broadcast booth, then higher
into the rites
of the front office,
your soul still roams the field,
combs it for hits
that never got through.
Your ear cocks
for that song: the body
raining hard on the basepath.

In Florida, when you pick up a bat,
the deep woods stir.
A practice swing and the river
jumps into your wrists.
You make good contact
with that world
you've seen from the moon.
As if the Yankees remember
your words: "A man lives on
in the life of others,"
they hand you a miracle; you sign.

What is lonely as one hit
in twelve at-bats?
Call it a rain dance
in the season of old bones,

your playing four games
while the trees grow back,
your fist, stone,
as you dream back your speed,
run faster than you can run.

Ryne Duren, Yankee Reliever

◆

As a nation sleeping under Ike
worshipped its image in the TV,
the real mirror was the
groggy one in your goggles —
something frightening returning
as a glare, as you swilled
your way toward the strike zone,
throwing at shoulders to find
the plate, practice pitches
crashing on the screen.

Rockwell's brushstroke
refused to wander;
the world never appeared so round.
In you we glimpsed
it was flat afterall
with places for falling.

For years the hitters slumbered,
their bats wilting in the sun.
Oh Ryne, how Ike's closed stances
positioned their feet
until your drunk fastballs
made them arch their backs and dance,
buzzing them alive when they'd count
their bodies in a flinch.

Before you fell into disfavor
and Kennedy was sworn in
and atom monsters swallowed up
a part of the sea,
once, before that,
when Ike was wearing

his white, white shoes
through the dark hallways of America,
you hurled a ball
which the eyes of the batter,
catcher, and umpire missed,
as if it were the 1950's
lost inside shadows —
a whole decade nobody saw.

John Updike

Tao in the Yankee Stadium Bleachers

◆

Distance brings proportion. From here
the populated tiers
as much as players seem part of the show:
a constructed stage beast, three folds of Dante's rose,
or a Chinese military hat
cunningly chased with bodies.
"Falling from his chariot, a drunk man is unhurt
because his soul is intact. Not knowing his fall,
he is astonished, he is invulnerable."
So, too, the "pure man" — "pure"
in the sense of undisturbed water.

"It is not necessary to seek out
a wasteland, swamp, or thicket."
The old men who saw Hans Wagner
scoop them up in lobster hands,
the opposing pitcher's pertinent hesitations,
the sky, this meadow, Mantle's thick baked neck,
the old men who in the changing rosters see
    a personal mutability,
green slats, wet stone are all to me
as when an emperor commands
a performance with a gesture of his eyes.

"No king on his throne has the joy of the dead,"
the skull told Chuang-tzu.
The thought of death is peppermint to you
when games begin with patriotic song
and a democratic sun beats broadly down.
The Inner Journey seems unjudgeably long
when small boys purchase cups of ice
and, distant as a paradise, experts, passionate and deft,
wait while Berra flies to left.

Robert Wallace

The Double Play

◆

In his sea lit
distance, the pitcher winding
like a clock about to chime comes down with

the ball, hit
sharply, under the artificial
banks of arc-lights, bounds like a vanishing string

over the green
to the shortstop magically
scoops to his right whirling above his invisible

shadows
in the dust redirects
its flight to the running poised second baseman

pirouettes
leaping, above the slide, to throw
from mid-air, across the colored tightened interval,

to the leaning-
out first baseman ends the dance
drawing it disappearing into his long brown glove

stretches. What
is too swift for deception
is final, lost, among the loosened figures

jogging off the field
(the pitcher walks), casual
in the space where the poem has happened.

Robert Penn Warren
He Was Formidable

◆

He was formidable, he was, the little booger,
As he spat in his hands and picked up the Louisville Slugger,
And at that bat-crack
Around those bases he could sure ball the jack,
And if from the outfield the peg had beat him home,
He would slide in slick, like a knife in a nigger.
So we dreamed of an afternoon to come,
In the Series, the ninth-inning hush, in the Yankee Stadium,
Sun low, score tied, bases full, two out, and he'd waltz to the plate with
his grin —
But no, oh no, not now, not ever! for in
That umpireless rhubarb and steel-heeled hugger-mugger,
    He got spiked sliding home, got spiked between the boxcars.

Oh, his hair was brown-bright as a chestnut, sun-glinting and curly,
And that lip that smiled boy-sweet could go, of a sudden, man-surly,
And the way he was built
Made the girls in his grade stare in darkness, and finger the quilt.
Yes, he was the kind you know born to give many delight,
And entering on such life-labor early,
Would have moved, bemused, in that rhythm and rite,
Through blood-throbbing blackness and moon-gleam
and pearly thigh-glimmer of night,
To the exquisite glut: *Woman Slays Self for Love*, as the tabloids would
tell —
But no, never now! Like a kid in his first brothel,
In that hot clasp and loveless hurly-burly,
    He spilled, as boys may, too soon, between the boxcars.

Or, he might have managed the best supermarket in town,
Bright with banners and chrome, where housewives push carts up and
down —

And morning and night
Walked the street with his credit *A*-rated and blood pressure right,
His boy a dentist in Nashville, his girl at State Normal;
Or a scientist flushed with *Time*-cover renown
For vaccine, or bomb, or smog removal;
Or a hero with phiz like hewn cedar, though young for the stars of a
                                                                    general,
Descending the steps of his personal plane to view the home-town
                                                                    unveiling.
But no, never now! — battle-cunning, the test tube, retailing,
All, all, in a helter-skeltering mishmash thrown
        To that clobber and grind, too soon, between the boxcars.

But what is success, or failure, at the last?
The newspaper whirled down the track when the through freight has
                                                                    passed
Will sink from that gust
To be of such value as it intrinsically must,
And why should we grieve for the name that boy might have made
To be printed on newsprint like that, for that blast
To whirl with the wheels' fanfaronade,
When we cannot even remember his name, nor humbly have prayed
That when the blunt grossness, slam-banging, bang-slamming, blots black
                                                                    the last blue flash of sky,
And our own lips utter the crazed organism's cry,
We may know the poor self not alone, but with all who are cast
        To that clobber, and slobber, and scream, between the boxcars?

Phillip Wedge

Satan Vows to Make a Comeback

◆

Yeah, they're sending me down to the lowest
of the low, some bush-league team, the Pandas.
I tell you it's a monopoly, man.
Isn't there some law against owning *all*
the teams? God is sure off base this time.
What's the point of having a World Series
if you're set up to lose from the outset?
We sure had them on the ropes though, didn't
we? Those Angels couldn't do it by themselves,
so God tells Christ to warm up in the pen.
Was that supposed to scare us or what? When
Belial, that great Sultan of Sloth,
came up — and the bases full — he slugged that
little old sphere clean out of the ballpark
to tie the game. And God lets Michael throw
one more pitch to Big Mammon the Cannon
and they're down by one with me up next. God
couldn't stand to be down by two in His
ballpark, especially not in the top
of the Ninth, my favorite number. So
he calls up the Super Star Himself to
pitch to me, saying, "J.C. can outshine
even Lucifer." I mean, where does He
get off saying that? What a spectacle
Christ made of Himself too. Only He would
need a Fiery Chariot instead
of just jogging in from the bullpen.
Why, those wheels of fire singed half the infield.
And then that s.o.G. sends the players
to the dugout and says He can do it
all Himself. Who does He think He is? God?
When I hit the first pitch downtown, what does
John Milton shout? Foul ball! If ever we

needed proof that umpires are blind as bats,
that was it. And of course I protested,
but God doesn't allow replays to change
a Judgment call. The game must remain pure.
     Naturally, I was really mad as Hell,
so when Christ tries to throw his thunderbolt
screwgie under my chin and I eat dust,
I have to charge the mound myself and kick
some dirt in His face. So His Immaculate
Self got soiled, so what? Milton kicks me out
of the game for that and we lose it all,
not only the Series but we're out of
the League for good, no comeback, no nothing.
     God thinks He has us down for good. Well, I've
got news for Him — the game's not over yet.
I'm talking Unions, man. All my boys
are behind me on this one; the system's
got to go. Once we get Adam and his
lot on our side, we've got God licked for sure.
The Union won't stand for less than equal
shares all round. Man, I'm talking Equity.

Charles B. Wheeler
Going to the Ballgame

◆

"PEEnuts, POP-CORN, CRACKerjax!"
A trochee, a spondee, and a dactyl
Shouted into the steamy evening air
By vendors prowling the stadium
Where the Fort Smith Twins,
Class "D," Cardinal farm club,
Played somebody from Oklahoma
Back in the thirties. The lights
Selected the bases, the mound,
And gestured toward the outfield,
Veiled with swarms of bugs
Pulled out of the southern darkness.
We parked behind the plate
On hard concrete steps,
My kid's narrow rump
Buffered with a folded sweater
In place of the rented cushion
Which would have cost us a dime.
The man with a megaphone
Bellowed the lineup twice,
Facing from third and from first,
And the players scattered to the field.
In their stations these grown men
Peppered the ball around
And crouched with hands on knees
Passing unintelligible encouraging
Remarks to one another, the pitcher
Spat over his shoulder and peered
At his target, a blur and a *thwump*
And the umpire signaled and my father shouted
And the other grown men around us
Joined the repartee, saying things
I sometimes didn't understand.

[119]

And so it went. I almost always
Lost sight of the ball beyond the infield
Because I hadn't yet got my glasses,
But there was no mistaking
The crack of the bat and the scurry
Of motion when a play was in progress.
My father leaned forward mostly
With his elbows on his knees,
The cuffs of his white business shirt
Folded twice backwards, a scorecard
Ready, and tried to explain to me
How you marked it — he came from the days
Of Cobb and Johnson and Wagner,
And at his dinky college
He'd lettered in all the sports.
He couldn't wisecrack the way
Other men in the stands could,
With self-satisfied guffaws
At especially telling points,
Making a ragged little drama
That counterpointed the ballgame,
But he shouted a lot and got mad
And made me ill at ease —
He seemed to think nobody
Ever played well, and I expect
That in class "D" they seldom did.
Anyway, I lived for the seventh inning
And my Dr. Pepper, easing the stiffness
While my father changed his chew
And clapped me on the shoulders,
Saying, "How do you like the game?"
I couldn't tell him, but I answered somehow.
I still don't know. Afterwards
We picked our way down the street
To his Chevy coupe, the katydids
Furiously chanting above us,
And rode home in silence.
He and my mother talked a long time in the bedroom.
I lay and listened to the thumping attic fan.

I think they had plans for me,
But if so I was never really told.

A lot of my time was spent
Dodging expectations, instinctively
Certain of my irrelevance.
Adults had made this game,
So let them play it.

The ship — that is, our house —
Plowed steadily through the night
On its unspecified errand,
Far out of sight of land, but comfortably
Provisioned against all anxieties,
The ocean breeze bellying the curtains
By my feet. And so I slept.
Next morning at the breakfast table,
Anchored firmly in the daylight,
I took up minor adventures
With my nose in the comic page
Of the *Southwest American*
While my father noisily finished
His shredded wheat, banged out of the door,
And started the Chevy. We never
Talked over the baseball game.
His car racketed up the driveway.
In a minute everything was quiet again.
My mother, turning from the window
Over the sink, said to me
"Well, what are you going to do today?"

Paul Zimmer

Thurman Dreaming in Right Field

◆

In right field I am so far out
The batter has unwound before
I hear the crack of his effort,
And the ball whirrs out and bounces
Like the wind off the wall
At idiot angles.
                    I am lonely
In that distance.
                    The moon shines
Like a long fly in right field
Where the rain falls first
And the snow drifts in the winter.
The sun cuts intricate shadows
From the decks above my head,
And balls, dropping like duck hawks,
Suddenly grow dull in the broken light
Of right field.
                    But there is
Always time for dreaming before
The impossible catch, the wheel
And shotgun throw on one bounce to
The plate, where the catcher slams
The ball onto the sliding runner's thigh,
And the crowd goes roaring, "Thurman!"
In that far field where
I am dreaming once again.

Thurman's Slumping Blues

◆

One day out in right field
The ball went by me quicker
Than a flushed-out quail.
I wagged my glove at it
But what I got was wind.
Then I fell down like a fool.
Fans stung me harder than
A swarm of bald-faced hornets.
That was what started
The whole damned thing.

I felt the sap run out of my knees,
Looked at my hands, they smelled of fish.
Wanda was up there in the box seats,
Sitting on a whole school of mackerel!

We dropped in the standings.
Pitchers pulled the string
And tied me up in knots.
I went left when I should have gone right.
Wanda commenced to acting skittish.

Today I woke up and she was gone.
Over my steak and eggs
The paper tells me that
This is last place.

Notes on the Contributors

◆

WILLIAM D. BARNEY lives in Fort Worth, Texas. He has written four books of poetry and has won a number of awards, including the Poetry Society of America's Robert Frost Memorial Award for a narrative poem in 1961. In 1982–83 he served as the Poet Laureate of Texas.

DAVID BOTTOMS teaches at Georgia State University. He has published several collections of poetry including *Shooting Rats at the Bibb County Dump* and *Under the Vulture Tree*. He co-edited, with Dave Smith, *The Morrow Anthology of Younger American Poets*, and has recently published two novels, *Any Cold Jordan* and *Easter Weekend*.

NEAL BOWERS teaches at Iowa State University and is editor of *Poet & Critic*. He is also the author of *James Dickey: The Poet as Pitchman* and he has published widely in magazines and journals.

RICK CAMPBELL is working on a doctorate in creative writing at Florida A & M University. His poems have appeared in *The Georgia Review*, *The Ohio Review*, *Cottonwood*, and many other magazines and journals.

DOUGLAS CARLSON lives in Fredonia, New York. His latest book is a collection of essays, *At the Edge*, from White Pine Press.

FRED CHAPPELL teaches at the University of North Carolina at Greensboro and is the author of many books of poetry and prose, the most recent being *First and Last Words* (poetry), and *Brighten the Corner Where You Are.*

TOM CLARK is the author of several books on baseball, including *Champagne and Baloney: The Rise and Fall of Finley's A's*, *Fan Poems*, *Baseball*, *One Last Round for the Shuffler: The Phil Douglas' Story*, and *No Big Deal* (with Mark Fidrych).

GREGORY CORSO has always been identified as one of the prime figures in the Beat Movement. In addition to publishing a novel and several plays, he has also published many collections of poetry, including *Herald of the Autochthonic Spirit* and *Selected Poems*. *Mindfield*, a collection from each of six earlier volumes, is his most recent publication.

MICHAEL CULROSS lives and works in Pasadena, California.

PHILIP DACEY teaches at Southwest State University in Marshall, Minnesota. He is the author of several books of poems, including *The Boy under the Bed* and *Gerard Manley Hopkins Meets Walt Whitman in Heaven and Other Poems*. *The Man with Red Suspenders* is his most recent collection of poems.

JIM DANIELS teaches at Carnegie Mellon University. His book *Places Everyone* won the 1985 Brittingham Prize. His most recent publication is a chapbook of baseball poems, *The Long Ball,* from Pig in a Poke Press.

GREGORY DJANIKIAN teaches at the University of Pennsylvania. His second book of poems is *Falling Deeply into America* from Carnegie Mellon Press.

RICHARD EBERHART holds the Pulitzer, Bollingen, and National Book Award prizes for poetry. His *New and Selected Poems 1930–1990* was published in 1990 by Blue Moon Press.

DAVID ALLEN EVANS teaches in the English department at South Dakota State University. He has published poems in magazines and journals throughout the country and is currently at work on a novel.

CHARLES FANNING teaches at Bridgewater State College in Bridgewater, Massachusetts. His *Exiles of Erin* won an American Book Award in 1989 and he has recently published *The Irish Voice in America,* a comprehensive study of the Irish-American literary experience.

ROBERT A. FINK is a professor of English at Hardin-Simmons University where he directs creative writing workshops. His poems have appeared in such magazines and journals as *Southern Poetry Review, Poetry Northwest,* and *Michigan Quarterly Review*. *The Ghostly Hitchhiker,* a collection of poems, appeared in 1989 from Corona Publishing Company.

SUSAN FIRER teaches creative writing at the University of Wisconsin — Milwaukee. Her collection *Life with the Tsar and Other Poems* was published by New Rivers Press.

[126]

ROBERT FRANCIS, now deceased, published many baseball poems during his productive life. His books include *Travelling in Amherst: A Poet's Journal, Come out into the Sun: Poems New and Selected*, and *The Orb Weaver*.

ROBERT GIBB teaches at Mount Union College in Alliance, Ohio. He has published seven volumes of poetry, the most recent of which, *Momentary Days*, won the Camden Award.

WALKER GIBSON is an emeritus professor of English at the University of Massachusetts — Amherst. He has written *Tough, Sweet and Stuffy: An Essay on Modern American Prose Styles* and nine other books including several collections of poetry.

GARY GILDNER has just published *The Warsaw Sparks*, an account of his coaching of a Polish baseball team in Warsaw. He teaches at Drake University.

JUDY GOLDMAN lives and writes in Charlotte, North Carolina. Her first collection of poetry, *Holding Back Winter*, is in its third printing. She has published over one hundred poems in numerous journals and magazines.

DONALD HALL taught English at the University of Michigan from 1957 until 1975; since then he has been a free-lance writer. In 1988 his book *The One Day* won the National Book Critics Circle Award in poetry. He lives in New Hampshire.

WILLIAM HEYEN teaches at the State University of New York at Brockport. An active member of the environmental movement and a widely published poet, his works include *Depth of Field, Erika: Poems of the Holocaust*, and *The Chestnut Rain*.

CONRAD HILBERRY teaches at Kalamazoo College. His most recent book of poems is *The Moon Seen as a Slice of Pineapple*. His new and selected poems, entitled *Sorting the Smoke*, was co-winner of the Iowa Poetry Prize for 1990.

JONATHAN HOLDEN teaches in the English department at Kansas State University. His collections of poems include *Falling from Stardom, Leverage*, and, most recently, *Against Paradise*.

RICHARD HUGO grew up in Seattle, served as a bombardier during World War II, and spent most of his teaching career at the University of Montana. *Making Certain It Goes On: The Collected Poems of Richard Hugo* was published in 1984, two years after his death.

JAMES HUMPHREY works nights in New York City helping the homeless find safe shelter. He counsels them as well as cooks for them. He lives with his wife in Hastings-on-Hudson, New York. In addition to *The Athlete* he has recently published *Ice*.

ROLFE HUMPHRIES is a classical scholar and translator of Juvenal, Lucretius, and Virgil, as well as the author of several collections of poetry.

RICHARD JACKSON teaches at the University of Tennessee — Chattanooga. He is the editor of *Poetry Miscellany* and is the author of two books of poetry, *Part of the Story* and *Worlds Apart*.

DON JOHNSON is the editor of *Aethlon: The Journal of Sport Literature*. He teaches at East Tennessee State University in Johnson City, Tennessee, and has published two collections of poems, *The Importance of Visible Scars* and *Watauga Drawdown*.

HALVARD JOHNSON lives and writes in New York City.

LAURENCE LIEBERMAN is the poetry editor at the University of Illinois Press. His most recent works are *The Mural of Wakeful Sleep* and *The Creole Mephistopheles*.

CAROL MASTERS is a poet and peace activist in Minneapolis, home of the Metrodome. She has spent too much time in jails not to mourn the loss of the sunshine of outdoor stadiums.

WILLIAM MATTHEWS was born in Cincinnati, Ohio. His many books of poems include *Ruining the New Road*, *Sleek for the Long Flight*, *Rising and Falling*, *Flood*, and *A Happy Childhood*. He teaches at Brooklyn College.

GAIL MAZUR is the founder and director of Blacksmith House Poetry Center in Cambridge, Massachusetts. She has published two books with David R. Godine Publishers, *Nightfire* and *The Pose of Happiness*. Her poems have appeared in magazines and journals throughout the country.

LINDA MIZEJEWSKI has an M.F.A. from the University of Arkansas and a Ph.D. in Critical and Cultural Studies from the University of Pittsburgh. Her essays and poetry have appeared in *Harper's*, *The Georgia Review*, *Southern Review*, and other journals. She teaches women's studies in the English department at Marquette University.

LARRY MOFFI is the author of two books of poems, *A Simple Progression* and *A Citizen's Handbook*. Formerly assistant director of the Cracker

Jack Old Timers Baseball Classic, he has served most recently as managing and associate editor of the book series *World of Baseball.*

LILLIAN MORRISON is the author of six books of poems and two anthologies related to sports — *Sprints and Distances,* and *Rhythm Road: Poems to Move to,* which was named a Notable Book for 1988 by the American Library Association.

TIM PEELER has published over thirty baseball poems, mostly in *Spitball.* He is the editor of *Synaesthesia* and also Third Lung Press. He has recently published *Preacher's Son* and *Civilizing the Savages.*

DONALD PETERSEN is a professor of English in the State University College at Oneonta, New York. His *The Spectral Boy (Poems 1948–1964)* was published by Wesleyan University Press. In the 1980s he published ten new poems and "The Legacy of Robert Lowell," an essay-review, in *The New Criterion.*

JACK RIDL teaches in the English department at Hope College in Holland, Michigan. He has written extensively on sports, and his most recent collection of poems is entitled *Between.*

MIKE SHANNON is editor and publisher of *Spitball,* the baseball literary magazine. He is the author of *Diamond Classics: Essays on One Hundred of the Best Baseball Books Ever Published* and of three chapbooks of baseball poetry, *The Mantle/Mays Controversy Solved, Pete Rose Agonistes,* and *Josh Gibson's Advice for Negro Catchers.*

TOM SHEEHAN has published two books of poems, *Ah, Devon Unbowed* and *The Saugus Book.* He lives in Saugus, Massachusetts.

ARTHUR SMITH teaches in the English department at the University of Tennessee — Knoxville. His *Elegy for Independence Day* won the Agnes Lynch Starrett Prize from the University of Pittsburgh Press in 1984.

DAVE SMITH is the editor of *Southern Review* and the author of nine books of poems, a novel, and a collection of short stories. His most recent collection of poems is *Cuba Night.*

R. T. SMITH is the poetry editor of the *Southern Humanities Review.* He has published several collections of poetry, including *Birch Light, Banish Misfortune,* and *From the High Dive.*

RON SMITH is chairman of the English department at St. Christopher's School in Richmond, Virginia. His poem "Running Again in the Hollywood Cemetery" won the 1986 Guy Owen Prize from the *Southern Poetry Review.*

DABNEY STUART teaches at Washington and Lee University in Lexington, Virginia, where he also edits *Shenandoah*. He is the author of several collections of poetry, the most recent of which is *Narcissus Dreaming* (Louisiana State University Press).

JAMES TATE teaches at the University of Massachusetts. His many collections of poems include *The Lost Pilot*, *The Riven Doggeries*, and *Absences*.

RODNEY TORRESON grew up on a farm in Iowa and currently lives in Grand Rapids, Michigan. His poems recently appeared in *Contemporary Michigan Poetry*.

JOHN UPDIKE has written a great deal of sports-related literature, including the *Rabbit* trilogy. Recent publications include *Hugging the Shore: Essays & Criticism*, *Roger's Version*, and *Trust Me*.

ROBERT WALLACE is a prolific writer whose work spans many genres from poetry to history. He teaches in the English department at Case Western Reserve University.

ROBERT PENN WARREN won Pulitzer Prizes in both fiction and poetry in his long and distinguished career.

PHILIP WEDGE teaches in the English department at the University of Kansas. He is also the poetry editor of *Cottonwood* magazine and Cottonwood Press. His poems have appeared in *The American Scholar*, *Aethlon, Stone Country*, and many other magazines and journals.

CHARLES B. WHEELER is a retired professor of English at the Ohio State University, author of *The Design of Poetry* (Norton, 1966) and co-author of *The Bible as Literature* (Oxford, 1986). He has recently published poems in *Hiram Poetry Review, Cumberland Poetry Review*, and *The Kansas Quarterly*.

PAUL ZIMMER is the poetry editor and director of the University of Iowa Press. His *The Great Bird of Love* was picked by William Stafford as one of the National Poetry Series winners in 1989.